THE GOD OF YES

"So many tend to look at God as a heavenly naysayer when He is really full of yeses. In his important book, THE GOD OF YES, Jud Wilhite shares ten life-changing principles that will transform your thinking and help you say yes to the life God wants you to have.

> —Craig Groeschel, author of *Alter Ego*,
> founding and senior pastor of Life Church

"THE GOD OF YES reads like a letter from a favorite friend. Jud is both wise and winsome. Since I've been on my own personal journey to live in God's yes this was a perfect resource that came at the perfect time. This book reinvigorated my passion, reminded me my contributions matter, and reignited my awareness to savor the small gifts. Don't just buy this book, dare to live its message!"

> —Lysa TerKeurst, author of *Unglued*,
> president of Proverbs 31 Ministries

"Life as a Christian is supposed to be freedom, not slavery, it's supposed to be exciting, not boring; it's supposed to be an adventure, not predictable; it's supposed to be 'yes,' not 'no.' Jud helps us see all the areas where we misunderstand God's freedom and live under self-imposed rules, all the while God is waiting for us to ask so that He can say 'yes.'"

> —Kyle Idelman, author of *Not a Fan* and *Gods at War*,
> teaching pastor at Southeast Christian Church

"Open this book and let Jud take you on a journey of spiritual discovery. You'll be encouraged, refreshed, challenged, inspired, and renewed. Don't delay—say 'yes' to the adventure that awaits."   —Lee Strobel, author of *The Case for Christ* and *The Case for Faith*

"Sometimes we can buy into the wrong notion that God is all about saying no to the things we desire in our life. Don't allow the wrong focus of who God is to prevent you from realizing all that He has planned for you. If you have forgotten that Jesus came to bring good news, that He has a plan for your life and loves you, then I hope you will read this book and open your life up to the extraordinary truth of God's 'yes' to you."   —Pete Wilson, author of *Let Hope In*, founding and lead pastor of Cross Point Church

The God of Yes

The God of
YES

Living in the Joy of His Complete Acceptance

JUD WILHITE

New York Boston Nashville

All Scripture quotations, unless otherwise indicated, are taken from the Holy Bible, New Living Translation, copyright © 1996, 2004. Used by permission of Tyndale House Publishers Inc., Carol Stream, Illinois 60188. All rights reserved.

Scripture quotations marked (ESV) are taken from The Holy Bible, English Standard Version, copyright © 2001 by Crossway Bibles, a division of Good News Publishers. Used by permission. All rights reserved.

Scripture quotations marked (MSG) are taken from The Message by Eugene H. Peterson. Copyright © 1993, 1994, 1995, 1996, 2000, 2001, 2002. Used by permission of NavPress Publishing Group.

Scripture quotations marked (NIV) are taken from the Holy Bible, New International Version. Copyright © 1973, 1973, 1984, by Biblica, Inc. Used by permission of Zondervan.

FaithWords
Hachette Book Group
1290 Avenue of the Americas
New York, NY 10104

www.faithwords.com

Printed in the United States of America

RRD-C

Originally published in hardcover by Hachette Book Group
First trade edition: February 2015

10 9 8 7 6 5 4 3 2 1

FaithWords is a division of Hachette Book Group, Inc.
The FaithWords name and logo are trademarks of Hachette Book Group, Inc.

The Hachette Speakers Bureau provides a wide range of authors for speaking events. To find out more, go to www.hachettespeakersbureau.com or call (866) 376-6591.

The publisher is not responsible for websites (or their content) that are not owned by the publisher.

Book design by Marie Mundaca

Library of Congress Cataloging-in-Publication Data
Wilhite, Jud, 1971-
The God of yes : how faith makes all things new / Jud Wilhite.
    pages cm
Includes bibliographical references.
ISBN 978-1-4555-1539-4 (hardcover) — ISBN 978-1-4789-2545-3 (audio download) — ISBN 978-1-4555-1538-7 (ebook) 1. Submissiveness—Religious aspects—Christianity. 2. Christian life. I. Title.
BV4647.A25W55 2014
248.4—dc23   2013016174

ISBN: 978-1-4555-1537-0 (pbk.)

Contents

Introduction
Just Say Yes

The oldest, shortest words—"yes" and "no"—are
those which require the most thought.

—*Pythagoras*

The contrast of flying into Las Vegas on Friday afternoon
and flying out on Sunday night is remarkable. Since Vegas is
my home, I've made both trips many times and the disparity
still amazes me. Most flights coming in for the weekend bring
a plane full of rowdy, excited people eager to blow off steam.
They're headed to Vegas to party, relax, gamble, shop, take in
the shows, and celebrate like there's no tomorrow.

These Friday flights are always sold out and packed tighter
than an overhead bin crammed with designer luggage. The
people chat and mingle as if the cocktail party has already
started. Sometimes you hear decks of cards being shuffled.
Everybody asks where everybody is going to stay, what shows
they will see, how many times they've been before, and their
favorite restaurants and casinos.

If they ask and find out I live in Vegas, they get intrigued. Usually my "I'm a pastor of a church" kills conversation on flights, but oddly for those flying into Vegas, the fact that I'm a pastor of a church with campuses in *Vegas* surprises them. I usually hear things like, "Now, there's an oxymoron—a Las Vegas pastor!" followed by lots of questions: "What's it like? Are there many churches in Vegas? How many celebrities have you met? What's the craziest thing that's ever happened at your church? Do you get poker chips in your offering?" After a while they usually conclude by saying, "There must be a lot of people in Vegas who need what you do," and then it's on to other things.

The flights leaving Vegas on Sunday night are just as packed as the ones coming in, but they're as quiet as a cemetery. I always know I can get lots of work done flying out on Sunday night. Most people won't even make eye contact with you, at least those who aren't wearing sunglasses. Many are wearing baseball caps or hats and are asleep before the plane doors shut. The laughter and inquisitiveness are gone, and there aren't many conversations with strangers flying out of Sin City on a Sunday night, although I have supplied Advil to a number of people.

FOR OR AGAINST

Living in one of the pleasure capitals of the world, I get a front row seat to many of the ways we try to fill our lives through entertainment. Vegas is wired up to max out pleasures at any moment. The lights are on 24/7 with non-stop shows, gaming, shopping, and food prepared by world-renowned chefs. Celebrities are always commemorating birthdays and corporate milestones as people roll in ready to spend money and enjoy themselves in ways that they would never do at home and are impossible to sustain.

Live here awhile and you learn that if someone stays long enough, plays long enough, and parties long enough, they always bottom out. Many times they turn to God for help and walk into our church. Over twenty years as a believer has taught me that often what we're looking for in the pursuit of pleasure is really something only God can provide.

Unfortunately, we tend to get the impression that God is mainly about saying no to things in life. Maybe we picked this up from church or someone's teaching we heard along the way. Or we see Christians who are constantly harping on other people to get it together, judging them for not living a more "Christian lifestyle."

Perhaps we had an encounter with someone yelling at people with a bullhorn on the sidewalk or holding a sign up about God's judgment. It could be for reasons we just don't understand, we feel guilty for enjoying things in life. We've let second parties shape our view of God more than the Bible and our firsthand experience of a relationship with Him.

If we only base our understanding of God on secondhand sound bites from others, we can be left with a general sense that God is anti-everything. He's anti-music, anti-movies, anti-dancing, anti-sex, anti-laughter, anti-fun, anti-Democrat or anti-Republican (depending on where you live), and the list goes on. He's pretty much anti-life!

But something is desperately wrong when our impression of God is mainly about things He is against, real or imagined, and not about what He is *for!* And please don't get me wrong: God is *against* plenty of sinful behaviors that we see expressed in the Bible, but He is *for* many more healthy ways of living, including real pleasure. Most certainly, He is *for* people to know Him and experience all of life—not as guilt but as gift.

NEW LEASE OR OLD LEASH

I realize living out of this view of God can take time. Long after I said yes to God in my life, I still doubted whether He said yes to me. I felt I'd never be good enough, never measure up, and never ultimately please Him. When you aren't convinced someone likes you, it makes it challenging to trust them with every aspect of your life. I feared God was the God of No. After all, don't the Ten Commandments say again and again, "Thou shalt *not*"? Isn't God mainly trying to get our attention to stop doing bad stuff? Doesn't God want to end the party and turn the music down?

There were a lot of negative consequences for the way this belief shaped my life. I saw my relationship with God in more negative than positive terms. My faith was boiled down to what I felt I was *not* doing. Consequently, I looked for joy in places other than God. Turning to hobbies, entertainment, books, and learning, all of which are good things, I sought a level of satisfaction from them that they could not ultimately sustain.

Similarly, I turned to pleasing people and seeking their approval, whether it was through a work project or a family achievement. And there was this nagging sense that I just wasn't cutting it. God was there and He put up with me, but deep down I still felt like He said *no* to me. So I compartmentalized my faith and my life. I loved God, but I also held back a lot of my heart. And it never occurred to me to look to Him as the ultimate source of joy in my life.

Can you relate? What has your experience with God been like up to now? I mean, does your faith ever feel less like a new *lease* on living and more like an old *leash*? As a believer, do you still feel like deep down God says no to you more than yes? Are you focused more on what to avoid rather than what to embrace? If something feels good, do you secretly sense it must be wrong? Have you reduced faith down to duty and responsibility more than joy and love?

The result of not fully understanding God's yes is a subtle drift in our heart from the One that we love. We starve ourselves from many of God's good gifts for a while, then engage in a binging and purging cycle with everything from food to shopping to church involvement, pursuits that are anything but healthy in their extremes. We keep trying to find lasting satisfaction in a relationship or an accomplishment or another dose of praise for the need for approval.

Just as visitors to Vegas soon discover that overstimulated pleasure doesn't satisfy them for long, we get frustrated with our attempts to find lasting satisfaction and grow weary. We begin to lose the ability to enjoy simple things, to laugh, to rest in God's love and be content with His provision. Maybe we even become one of those grumpy, angry, negative Christians we thought we'd never become, judging others so we can feel better about ourselves.

A root issue in all of these things is that we are not fully embracing God's yes to every part of our life and world. Think about it for a moment. Imagine enjoying God thoroughly and as a by-product celebrating food, sex, work, marriage, meaningful relationships with our kids, helping others, and living in contentment before Him. All of these things are gifts from God and are given for our enjoyment. We simply have to stop treating our pursuit of meaning and satisfaction like a weekend trip to Vegas.

OVER THE MOON OR UNDER THE SUN

To explore God's yes to all of life, we'll turn to what some perceive to be the ultimate "no" book of the Bible. Ecclesiastes reads like Solomon's personal journal entries, a diary in which he pulls no punches looking at life. Almost every page describes his attempts to find pleasure in the extremes of life, taking something good like laughter or work, and then going too far, "over the moon," only to find that it doesn't satisfy him. He realizes that there's "nothing new under the sun," and there must be more to this life than just the pursuit of physical pleasure.

When I first studied Ecclesiastes in college, the book struck me like a lightning rod, reinvigorating my faith. I found myself nodding in agreement at times, shrugging in bewilderment, and sometimes turning away in frustration. The whole experience of wrestling with the book led me into a deeper connection to God. Initially, it had pointed me to hope during a time when I was drowning in the mire of contemporary philosophy.

In graduate school I majored in both theology and philosophy and immersed myself in the writings of everyone from Nietzsche and Heidegger to Foucault and Derrida. In their own ways, these thinkers were questioning the foundations of everything and leading me to reconsider so much of what I had taken for granted—even basic concepts like good and evil, reality and perception, motive and behavior.

In this confusion, wrestling with feelings of meaninglessness and purpose, trying to find my way in the world, I opened Ecclesiastes and it was like a healing ointment. Here was someone facing the harsh edges of life bluntly, profoundly, and honestly, even if at times confusingly. This wasn't a message that life was all lollipops and rainbows; this was straightforward, from-the-gut, well-seasoned meat for a starving soul. Solomon brings no illusions to the harsh edges of life. He delivers truth with a blow that ultimately God used to save me a lot of years of wandering.

Reading Ecclesiastes over the years since then has only reinforced my understanding and appreciation of it. I'm convinced Solomon's journey in this book represents a roundabout "yes" to God and every aspect of life. It provides a framework for a faith that squares off with reality and finds it infused with meaning. Some have gone so far as to see Ecclesiastes as similar to the book of Philippians, the book of joy, in the New Testament. What Ecclesiastes shows us so powerfully is that if we take our eyes off God, eventually things begin to wither in our lives. But when we say yes to Him and live in His yes to us, we experience revitalization.

YES OR NO

My life changed radically when I first said yes to God, but it changed ultimately when I lived in the implications of God's yes to me, something that Ecclesiastes helped me fully embrace. As I began to grow and understand what God was *for*, I discovered the secret to a spiritually rich life: saying yes to God in each moment and living in the incredible yes God declares to me in Jesus.

Check out how Paul puts it: "For all of God's promises have been fulfilled in Christ with a resounding 'Yes!'" (2 Corinthians 1:20). Not some, not a few, but *all* of God's promises are fulfilled in Jesus. He's our salvation, our hope, and through Him, God not only fulfilled all the requirements of the law, but gave us a new identity and an inheritance that will never fade. We can live new lives in the joy of God's work in Jesus. He's shown in Jesus that He is pro-love, pro-forgiveness, pro-enjoyment, pro-purpose, and pro-life in the fullest and richest sense imaginable.

In the following pages, we'll look at many areas of life that God is for and see how we can discover satisfaction within them. First, we'll see that saying yes to God allows us to begin again to live in His affirmation of all of life as a gift. Everything is a spiritual opportunity for worship. We experience pleasure as more gift than threat and we celebrate it under God. Work becomes less of a burden and more of a mission to be engaged. Accomplishment finds its place not in accolades and achievements in themselves, but in living with wisdom before God. We discover the secret of contentment, live with eternity in perspective, and embrace joy in the small stuff.

In *The God of Yes*, I'll share how we can replace feelings of frustration with a vital spirituality that gives fulfillment; break destructive beliefs about God so that you can lead a more joyful life; embrace God's yes to all of life and experience more satisfaction at work and at home; and discover contentment in any season of life so you experience all that God has for you today. It is incredible news: God has declared a massive *Yes!* over your life in Jesus.

If you are frustrated and feeling empty, tired, and frayed, things can change in your life tomorrow even if your circumstances don't. The restlessness and discontent can be quieted in surrender before God. You can experience God's satisfaction in the small and large things, in life and love, in your relationships and in your work. You'll find something much more fulfilling and longer lasting than any weekend to Vegas—or anywhere else—could provide.

You'll discover that by saying yes to God, you can live in God's yes to you!

Chapter One
Yes to God

He who has a why to live for, can bear almost any
how.

—Nietzsche

Recently, I was scheduled to call in for a live radio interview
with a national audience. This was a big interview and one I
was excited about participating in. To get the best phone sig-
nal with the least interference, the radio station requested I
call in on a landline. I had every intention of doing so, but
found myself driving back from an appointment and running
late. I had met with someone who was really hurting, and we
had one of those conversations where you can't just get up
and leave because the clock says so.

About ten miles from my office, when I realized I wasn't
going to make it in time, I pulled off the freeway and found
a nice quaint park that was completely vacant. I parked next
to a Dumpster toward the back in a small parking lot. There
were no other cars and no people. It was perfect. The weather

was gorgeous for a fall day and the park was beautiful and quiet. I'd make the call from my cell phone and no one would be the wiser.

I dialed the station and began the interview. I was having a blast sharing about the Christian faith and what it means to me to be a follower of Jesus. After a few minutes a large green Sparkletts truck loaded with dozens of five-gallon water bottles pulled into the empty parking lot and began to back in right next to my car. Its engine was humming, the gears and brakes were screeching, and then the beep...beep... beep...beep of reverse. It was all so...*loud*. I couldn't believe it, but cupped my hand over the phone and sighed in frustration.

Not five minutes later, an ice cream wagon (converted from an old Chevy truck) pulled into the parking lot playing a bad ice cream wagon jingle through a huge loudspeaker. It sounded like an off-version of the *Jeopardy!* theme song cranked up to rock concert volume.

As soon as that blaring jingle was out of hearing range, which felt like twenty minutes, I heard the massive churning of another truck. I looked up and saw a city garbage truck coming straight for me. *Unbelievable!*

The one time all week he would be on this route and would lift this Dumpster was when I parked next to it on a live national radio interview! There was nothing I could do. Starting my car would be too distracting and I was worried about dropping the call if I drove away. Of course, what could be louder than a dump truck picking up a Dumpster right beside me?

It sounded like I was in a war zone as the driver rattled the metal Dumpster; the clanging of steel and trash echoed off everything. When the dump truck finally pulled away, I took a deep breath. Then the Sparkletts truck fired off his big engine and decided his lunch break was over. *Seriously?* He ground the gears and pulled away.

Finally, I thought I would have a moment's peace, only to hear the ice cream truck approaching again, horrendous jingle and all. *Are you kidding me? What was he thinking?* There were no kids the first time. There were no people anywhere. *Why would there be now?*

By the time he made his *slow* U-turn and pulled away, my interview was wrapping up. I had little idea of what I'd actually said with everything going on around me. I sensed the host was not happy. When I hung up, I sat there exhausted. And I realized the park was now completely quiet. Nothing was moving. Not a single sound anywhere. It was like the circus had rolled in, unloaded the trapeze artists, jugglers, elephants, and tigers who performed their acts, only to pull out without leaving a trace. I let out a deep, long sigh of frustration, knowing I had completely bombed the interview.

THE SIGHS OF LIFE

When was the last time you let out a huge sigh of frustration? You know, a *Napoleon Dynamite* kind of sigh? Maybe it's when you hit gridlock on the freeway; when you realize your only set of keys are in the car just as you shut the locked door; when you hear one child say, "Mom, brother just went potty in the bathtub!" When you get stuck in the middle seat of an airplane between two big guys and one of them has a sleeveless shirt, needs deodorant, and keeps adjusting the overhead air—sigh.

We all feel this way sometimes—like our life is lived from one long sigh to the next. Waiting on the next thing to go wrong, we get frustrated. There was a time for some of us when the romance was new. We were so happy running through the fields to the sound of music. Love was in the air. Now, something else is in the air, and it doesn't smell like love.

Once upon a time at work, things were fresh and exciting, filled with possibilities for a profitable and bright future. Now it feels tedious and exhausting, like you're doing your time while hanging on by the skin of your teeth. For some, school was once a new adventure; now it feels like survival and you're trying hard to stay engaged enough to get to graduation. Hobbies start out fun, from sports to scrapbooking to video games to working out, but over time they don't feel so new anymore. Pretty soon the gym is just a building that mocks you on the way home from work—LOSER! (Or maybe that's just me.)

Sometimes things not only feel tired, but can start to feel hopeless. We wonder where we'll find the energy to hang on, to push through and keep all the plates spinning and to hold it all together. All of this gets wrapped up and expressed in our sighs of frustration.

This is where Solomon finds himself in the book of Ecclesiastes. He begins the book with the conclusion of his quest to find satisfaction and substance apart from God. This was typical of this kind of ancient Hebrew literature. He writes, "These are the words of the Teacher, King David's son, who ruled in Jerusalem. 'Everything is meaningless,' says the

Teacher, 'completely meaningless! What do people get for all their hard work under the sun?'" (Ecclesiastes 1:1–3).

Solomon is worn out. He's tired, depressed, and emotionally spent. He begins with a statement of his despair. Life lived "under the sun"—with no regard for the God beyond the sun—has come up empty. The word translated as "meaningless" can have the literal sense of a sigh, that deep exhale of frustration and exhaustion that we've all experienced. In fact, "meaningless" could also be translated "breath," "mist," or "vapor," basically anything without enduring substance.

Like a mist that rises from the ground in the morning and disappears in the sun, so is all that Solomon experienced without God. It is passing, it is like "chasing the wind," he says. He goes on to chronicle all the places he sought substance apart from God—building projects, sensual pleasures, lavish parties, entertainment, wisdom, work, accomplishment, wealth, education, you name it. Everything had lost its appeal. It's all mist and vapor. It all comes down to nothing. *Sighhhh.*

WHEN EVERYTHING IS NOTHING

If you know much about Solomon in the Bible, then you're wondering how he got to this level of burnout. What happened? Solomon was the third king of Israel, the son of David who was known as a man after God's own heart. Solomon's father was full of faith and this would have been a key part of his growing up years. He was born into wealth, royalty, and a family filled with opportunity, belief, and hope.

Solomon had walked with God, and God had even mani-

fested Himself to him on two occasions (1 Kings 11:9). He
built the Temple for God that his father, David, had only
dreamed about. When you read through Solomon's prayer as he
dedicated the completed Temple to God, you sense his passion
and devotion (1 Kings 8:23–53). He's saying yes to God and
living in God's yes.

When we compare and contrast that commitment with
his observations in the book of Ecclesiastes, we're shocked
by a tragic and radical shift. The passion for God is gone,
exchanged for irritation and anguish. The joy of faith is re-
placed with a miserly view of life and a distant perspective
of God. The Bible doesn't leave us guessing about what happened. A couple chapters after Solomon's incredible prayer
of dedication, we read that he married many foreign wives
and in "Solomon's old age, they turned his heart to worship
other gods instead of being completely faithful to the LORD
his God, as his father, David, had been" (1 Kings 11:4).

Solomon drifted into the worship of other gods and eventually tried to find satisfaction in nothing but material things.
His story is not the celebrity biography of a guy who lived a
crazy life of wealth and decadence only to became a believer
and live to tell his "sex, drugs, and rock and roll" conversion
story.

This is the journey of a guy who worshipped God and followed Him for many years, but drifted farther and farther
from his relationship with Him. He distanced himself from
the life God desired for him. In a context of Christianity,
we'd say this is the story of someone who grew up in church,
prayed to become a believer, and walked the aisle at church
as a young person. He lived a committed life of faith for

decades, but later in life he wandered. He moved from saying yes to God, to a hesitant maybe, to an eventual no. And now writing Ecclesiastes, it's like he's coming back to his senses, thinking on the page and processing all he's experienced. Bottom line, he realizes that life under the sun, apart from God, has no purpose.

What we see in the opening verses of Ecclesiastes is living proof that *Everything – God = Nothing*. All the wealth, accomplishments, parties, wisdom, and books that Solomon experienced amounted to nothing apart from God. These can be wonderful gifts enjoyed under God, but they make a bad replacement for God.

Thousands of years later, Søren Kierkegaard, the Danish philosopher, would look out at his day and come to similar conclusions: "I saw that the meaning of life was to make a living, its goal to become a councilor, that the rich delight of love was to acquire a well-to-do girl, that the blessedness of friendship was to help each other in financial difficulties, that wisdom was whatever the majority assumed it to be, that enthusiasm was to give a speech...that piety was to go to communion once a year. This I saw, and I laughed."[1] Kierkegaard wasn't laughing because it was hilarious but because it was absurd to think that those things equaled real meaning in life.

The great news is that God's math is different: *God + Nothing = Everything*. No matter how empty and messed up things seem around you, they are transformed when you invite God into them. Even if you are in a job you don't really like; in a waiting room you wish you weren't in; in a relationship you don't understand; waiting for a partner you're doubting will ever come along, there can be joy. I'm not saying these things aren't excruciatingly hard, but with God front and center in our lives, we can face them and find meaning in them nevertheless.

We see that the final word of Solomon's life experiment ends in an affirmation. He concludes Ecclesiastes by saying: "That's the whole story. Here now is my final conclusion: Fear God and obey his commands, for this is everyone's duty" (12:11). In the original language, it implies that fearing and obeying God make up the "whole person." Life under God, lived in reverent fear or respect for God, is life under God's yes. When we live like *God + Nothing = Everything,* we are in a position to discover God's purpose in every day, which is that we live for Him and enjoy Him. We wake up to the meaning that He infuses into every moment.

Ecclesiastes is a message for believers, a bold reminder from one who has wandered far from faith and is making his way back. As Samuel Johnson, the famous English author, once wrote: "People need to be reminded more often than they need to be instructed," and Solomon does both powerfully.[2] He reminds us of the slow and deadly way we can take our eyes off God. It begins almost imperceptibly. We are strong and secure in our faith. We begin to live in God's blessings and reap the benefits of trusting Him and walking faithfully with Him over time. In that comfort we get distracted and busy. We no longer discipline ourselves to live toward God as purposefully. We stop reading our Bibles as often, pray less, attend church more sporadically, and can't remember the last new thing we learned about God.

We say yes to God's forgiveness, but we slide into no on forgiving others who have hurt us; yes to following Him, but no to letting go of a destructive sin or addiction that keeps us from Him; yes to church, but no to personally owning our faith outside of church attendance; yes to God's love for us, but no to loving those not like us; yes to His blessing toward us, but no to blessing others; yes to eternal life, but no to the life He desires for us today.

Maybe like Solomon, we have friends or family who don't share our faith, and we've allowed them to influence us to the point of apathy toward the things of God. These decisions can add up cumulatively and we can find ourselves drifting, not intentionally. But before we know it, we wake up one day and have traveled far from loving God with all our heart. Life gets reduced to a sigh of tedium, of weariness, of resignation.

We can also be tempted to shove religious things into our lives as a substitute for God. We try to cram the approval and respect of others who see us at church, our positive feelings from being involved in kind acts, our morality into our lives to satisfy what only God can satisfy. We focus more on the outside than the inside. This was how the religious leaders lived in Jesus' day. They kept up all the appearances, but inside they had drifted far from God. He called them "whitewashed tombs." They looked great on the outside, but on the inside they were filled with "dead people's bones and all sorts of impurity" (Matthew 23:27). We must return to God to have change in our lives from the inside out.

ENOUGH IS NEVER ENOUGH

When I was a kid, the phrase I used most often around the house was, "I'm bored." I would mope around and wear my parents out. Maybe that is why I have so little patience for my kids when they use it today. They know my reply: "Your boredom is not my responsibility. You are responsible for your boredom, and you'll never have as much free time in your life as you do now." (Yes, I sound just like my mother!) They've heard it so often they repeat the last part of it with me. It drives them crazy! If they keep moping around, I tell them, "Since you are so bored, why don't you clean the kitchen or mow the yard?" This always gets an exasperated moan and ends the conversation.

We all face the daily routine of life and sometimes it begins to feel like the same ole, same ole. We get bored. Solomon notes the constant monotony of life: "Generations come and generations go, but the earth never changes. The sun rises and the sun sets, then hurries around to rise again. The wind blows south, and then turns north. Around and around it goes, blowing in circles. Rivers run into the sea, but the sea is never full. Then the water returns again to the rivers and flows out again to the sea. Everything is wearisome beyond description. No matter how much we see, we are never satisfied. No matter how much we hear, we are not content" (Ecclesiastes 1:4–8).

Can you feel the monotony? You get up, go through the day, come home, go to bed, and wake up to do it all over again. Humans are continually coming and going while the earth is repetitively remaining the same. There is no conceivable end to the problem of earthly futility. The sun rises and sets, the wind blows, the streams flow. It's just the same ole, same ole.

The ancient Greek skeptics conceived history as circular.

This means that history has no definite point of beginning or termination. It goes around and around in an endless, meaningless, vicious circle of insignificance. Yet the first statement recorded in Genesis stands against this view of life and history: "In the beginning God created…" (1:1). We see that a starting point to history is found, not in chaos as a cosmic accident, but through a purposeful act by a creator God. History is seen as linear, going somewhere with a purpose.

This view of history and life is anchored in living toward the God who set it in motion. Science examines the movements of the sun, wind, and streams and notes what they do. But science can never tell us the overarching purpose of why the sun rises and sets. Stephen Hawking, for years Lucasian Professor of Mathematics at Cambridge University, concluded that science must be content to explain the "what" of human observations, God is the only one able to answer the "why."[3] And Solomon is asking the why questions.

THE ANTIDOTE TO BOREDOM

What we need in the daily grind is a fresh vision of God! When we say yes to God and invite Him into the monotony of life, we experience the antidote to boredom. We hear the same old alarm and walk to the same old bathroom and pick up the same old toothbrush, but in our heart we give thanks to God for the gift of another day, for a bathroom to get ready in, for a toothbrush to use.

We eat the same old breakfast, but we celebrate that God provides even our cereal while many in the world don't have the luxury of breakfast. We get in the same old car and appreciate the ride. We go to the same old job looking forward to serving God at work. We celebrate Him and remember many would love to have a job at all. We walk in at the end of the day and kiss our spouse and rejoice in the companionship God provides. This God of order, surprise, and beauty can transform the same ole in our lives. We can welcome Him into our every day and He can make all things new.

The same stuff we did yesterday can be different today when done in light of the resurrection of Jesus. After the lengthiest discussion of the resurrection and all it means in the Bible, Paul concludes his discussion: "So, my dear brothers and sisters, be strong and immovable. Always work enthusiastically for the Lord, for you know that *nothing you do for the Lord is ever useless*" (1 Corinthians 15:58). Because Jesus rose from the dead, everything we do takes on a new meaning.

He doesn't qualify it. Every act of kindness, goodness, and love; every moment teaching a child or encouraging someone else; every time you make food for a friend in crisis, or give your best at your job, all of it matters if you do it for God. Everything counts.

THIS IS YOUR WAKE-UP CALL

Solomon's memoir in Ecclesiastes reads like someone waking up from many years of being asleep to God's Word and will. And people do and say all kinds of crazy things in their sleep. I remember one night looking over at my wife, Lori, sleeping with her arm straight up in the air like some crazy Nazi salute for no reason. It didn't look comfortable, so I gently put it down.

When we are asleep to God, we're not aware of what we're missing or even the effects of what we're doing. Hit the snooze button long enough and even the possibility of waking up and experiencing new life can seem far-fetched. Solomon looked out in frustration at how nothing changes: "History merely repeats itself. It has all been done before. Nothing under the sun is truly new. Sometimes people say, 'Here is something new!' But actually it is old; nothing is ever truly new. We don't remember what happened in the past, and in future generations, no one will remember what we are doing now" (Ecclesiastes 1:9–11).

When we first read these words, they seem outdated at best, false at worst. What does he mean there is nothing new, that all has already been? We have circled the moon and split the atom. In a hundred years we have gone from horse and buggy, to cars, refrigerators, microwaves, computers, not to mention the inventions in the last couple of millennia such as irrigation, agriculture, the printing press, and the clock. What in the world is he talking about: "Nothing new under the sun"?

Surely he knew there were new things—Solomon was considered the wisest man on earth. He knew that things changed, but what he emphasizes is the laws that govern things and the behavior of people really don't change. There is a great difference in the way Attila the Hun killed with a sword and the way it is done today with high-tech equipment and nuclear weapons—but the behavior pattern is the same. Murder, envy, domination, these do not change. We have a lot of new gadgets and gear, but we have not been able to change ourselves. There is a resignation here, even a sense that Solomon has given up on whether change is really possible.

Yet all throughout the Bible we're reminded of the way God brings new life. He wants to do a new thing in our hearts and lives as we follow Him in faith. He wants to reveal Himself to us more and relate to us as our God. This is why the first Christians gathered and sang an Easter song to encourage one another. The song is quoted in Ephesians 5:14: "Awake, O sleeper, rise up from the dead, and Christ will give you light." This was a song for believers who needed to be reminded on a regular basis to stop hitting the snooze button and wake up, rise up spiritually, and allow Christ to give them light.

We wake up by living with a conscious awareness of God in everything in our lives. As philosopher and novelist G. K. Chesterton put it, "You say grace before meals. All right. But I say grace before the concert and the opera, and grace before the play and pantomime, and grace before I open a book, and grace before sketching, painting, swimming, fencing, boxing, walking, playing, dancing and grace before I dip the pen in the ink."[4] God was not an afterthought at mealtime, but the central focus throughout all the things he faced in the day. This is what it means to live in God's yes.

Has your initial yes to God become more like a maybe and eventually slipped into a no by default? Do you feel distant from God and see the effects and discontent all around you? Possibly you've started to believe that you can find lasting satisfaction in other things and you've turned there and begun to make those things ultimate. Just one more drink, one more TV show to escape, one more package of Oreos, one vacation on the credit card, one more product, one more conversation to avoid, one more of whatever you do or say, eat, drink, accomplish, or avoid to not have to wake up.

Do you sense God calling you to reconcile with someone or something from the past? Is there something there that you know He's leading you to deal with? Every time you think of it or feel convicted, you hit the snooze button and go back to sleep. "Just ten more minutes, please, I'm not ready to get up and deal with that."

Anxiety and worry may have you tied up in knots. You know that you're supposed to give your worry to God and trust Him with it, but you keep taking it back. You've grown more comfortable with the worry than the uncomfortable thought of giving it to God. You're hitting snooze instead of waking up to your life and moving forward.

The good news is that it's not too late. God is cheering you on with a resounding yes in Jesus! He desires for you to experience the richness of life lived in His yes. Say yes to His power in your life to change old habits and hang-ups. Say yes to His love for you again. Say yes with a sigh, but not a sigh of frustration, a sigh of relief as He takes on all your no's. Live again in God's yes to you. This is your wake-up call, right here and right now.

"Awake, O sleeper, rise up from the dead, and Christ will give you light."

Chapter Two
Yes to Pleasure

Love, and do what you will.

—*Saint Augustine*

Living in Las Vegas, I've definitely met some characters and had some "only in Vegas" type moments. One of them occurred on a weekend at Central Christian Church, the church I serve. As everyone was pulling onto the church property, a woman that we had tried to help many times decided to protest the church on the corner with a sign. People protesting at churches is not really news anymore and we had faced this before. Yet what struck me this time was what her sign said. In bright homemade letters on white poster board, it read: JUD WILHITE SMOKES WEED. I am not making this up! All weekend as people entered our church lot, this woman stood there with a sign that said I use drugs.

Truthfully, all I knew to do was laugh at the ridiculousness of it—only in Vegas! Everyone who has been at Central very long knows my story. I came to faith out of a four-year drug addiction, and in that period I smoked a *lot* of weed. This past year in front of hundreds of people in our church at our recovery ministry, I went forward and received my twenty-four-year sobriety chip! I am so grateful for the grace of God and for our church community, which has been a healing place for me and so many others. I know personally about the path of drugs and other ways that we seek to fill our lives with pleasure. I've learned the hard way that ultimately only God can satisfy the deepest longings of our heart.

IF IT FEELS GOOD

We all want to be happy and we all seek pleasure in something; the only difference is the path we take. Some seek pleasure in entertainment, approval, or exercise. Some get caught up with repetitive pleasurable habits that become addictions, whether illegal drugs, alcohol, prescription pills, parties, overeating, or too much shopping—you name it. The desire for pleasure and happiness is a powerful force. It leads us to buy things, say things, eat things, and do things. It's like an itch that has to be scratched.

Curiously enough, Dr. David Linden, professor of neuroscience at John Hopkins University, notes that everything from prayer to shopping, gambling, sex, and running all trigger the same interconnected brain areas. He writes in *The Compass of Pleasure:* "Using a brain scanner, it has now become possible to observe activation of the brain's pleasure circuitry in humans. Not surprisingly, this circuit is activated by 'vice' stimuli: orgasm, sweet and fatty foods, monetary reward, and some psychoactive drugs. What's surprising is that many behaviors that we consider virtuous have similar effects. Voluntary exercise, certain forms of meditation or prayer, receiving social approval, and even donating to charity can all activate the human pleasure circuit. *There's a neural unity of virtue and vice—pleasure is our compass, no matter what path we take.*[5] I find it remarkable that both virtue (good, healthy, and spiritual acts) and vice (potentially destructive and sinful acts) all trigger the same pleasure areas of the brain.

Dr. Robert Galbraith Heath, once chair of the Department of Psychiatry and Neurology at Tulane University, performed some studies that were later considered unethical in the middle part of the twentieth century. His goal was to help people with psychiatric disorders by stimulating the brain with implanted electrodes.

The electrodes were placed into the brains of several individuals. After three months of healing, researchers began to stimulate certain brain areas and allow the patients themselves to control stimulation. When a male patient was given the chance to self-stimulate the pleasure area of his brain, he returned to it again and again to the exclusion of everything else. Another woman "self-stimulated throughout the day, neglecting her personal hygiene and family commitments. A chronic ulceration developed at the tip of the finger used to adjust the amplitude dial and she frequently tampered with the device in an effort to increase the stimulation amplitude."[6]

It's almost as if we can't stop ourselves from returning to something that gives us that pleasurable surge. However, the challenge with pleasure is that no matter how much we scratch, the itch always comes back. No matter how much we achieve, connect, entertain ourselves, or increase the amplitude, we are never, ever satisfied. Where do we find the most lasting pleasure that brings pleasure to God? Despite what many might tell you, it's not in a Vegas casino.

THE GOOD LIFE

Solomon would've been right at home in Las Vegas considering the way he threw himself into pleasures of every kind to find lasting satisfaction. He did his own version of an extended party weekend. He writes: "I said to myself, 'Come on, let's try pleasure. Let's look for the "good things" in life'" (Ecclesiastes 2:1).

Rather than turn to a trusted friend or mentor for insight into how to live, he tells himself "YOLO—you only live once. Go for it!" This reminds us of the deceitfulness of the human heart and how it often leads us astray. Solomon goes on to tell us what he did: "I collected great sums of silver and gold, the treasure of many kings and provinces. I hired wonderful singers, both men and women, and had many beautiful concubines. I had everything a man could desire! So I became greater than all who had lived in Jerusalem before me, and my wisdom never failed me. Anything I wanted, I would take. I denied myself no pleasure" (Ecclesiastes 2:8–10).

Solomon lived the marketed Vegas lifestyle to the hilt. He went big, buying everything he wanted, having the best entertainment, the best food, the best parties, and the best sex. He enjoyed everything a person could desire at the instant he desired it. "I never said no to myself," he writes, "I gave in to every impulse, held back nothing" (Ecclesiastes 2:10 MSG). As an example, he had 300 wives and 700 concubines to indulge every kind of sexual pleasure. If he came to Vegas, he would need one whole wing of the Mirage just for his ladies!

He indulged every appetite in the search for satisfaction. He said, "I decided to cheer myself with wine" (Ecclesiastes 2:3). His memoir mentions careful thought put into this. Solomon isn't just out to get plastered, but to walk the line that brings the most pleasure. He turned to music and had the best singers and musicians of his day perform and play. He built lavish buildings and enjoyed comedians and performers of the day, all intended to make him laugh. Yet in the end, reducing life to only what one can see, taste, and touch failed to satisfy. He writes: "But I found that this, too, was meaningless. So I said, 'Laughter is silly. What good does it do to seek pleasure?'" (Ecclesiastes 2:1–2).

Solomon sought pleasure for his own sake, motivated out of self-indulgence and self-gratification. He subjected all things—nature, people, possessions—to giving himself pleasure. He made pleasure ultimate and it failed him. As Mick Jagger of the Rolling Stones would put it a few thousand years later, he couldn't get no satisfaction.

The word "pleasure" in these verses comes from a Hebrew word meaning "joy" and "gladness." Throughout the Bible, pleasure is seen both as a danger and a gift from God. Paul warns of those who "love pleasure rather than God" (2 Timothy 3:4). Pleasure can lead us down a path of sin and disobedience to God. If you base your life and happiness on

the pursuit of pleasure, it leads to a lot of regret, meaninglessness, and ultimately dissatisfaction. Too much of even a good
thing is still too much.

Solomon's example makes it clear that this human struggle
with pleasure was nothing new. In fact, there are two schools
of philosophy mentioned directly in the Bible: the Stoic and
the Epicurean. In Acts, we read that Stoic and Epicurean
philosophers began to dispute with the apostle Paul in
Athens, Greece (17:18). Both of these groups were involved
in the pursuit of pleasure, but they were bitter enemies. They
were both skeptics about absolute truth and were concerned
with how we can be happy.

The Stoics held to a type of fatalism where all was prede-
termined. Life was based on logic and virtue, and external
things were not to have any impact, whether pleasure or
pain. The Epicureans sought happiness in hedonism, the
max of pleasure and the avoidance of pain. If it feels good,
then it is good, and if it hurts, then obviously it is bad.
The goal of life is to experience happiness. They ran into
the catch-22 of pleasure: if you achieve your pleasure goals,
you become bored, but if you don't satisfy your desires, you
remain frustrated. So people are basically trapped to some
degree in boredom or frustration. They sought to find the
balance in temperance.

In both of these schools of philosophy, we see the pursuit
of pleasure as a means of coping with life. Thankfully, the
Bible offers another way to consider pleasure and pain and
has a lot of wisdom to share on how to get the most and
best out of life. We were created to desire pleasure, and we
experience the most pleasure by rejoicing in God and enjoy-

ing everything in life as His creation. In this sense, God says
yes to pleasure.

IT'S ALL GOOD

When I first became a Christian, I could not see God's yes
as it relates to pleasure. Having come out of several years of
addiction, I had personally experienced the emptiness of pleasure apart from God. In my intense desire to clean up and
straighten out, I needed to say no to a lot of what I had embraced.

But I also subtly projected this no into other areas of my
life. I assumed that God didn't really want me to have fun, to
laugh, to experience joy in the simple pleasures found in food
and people. I expanded God's no far beyond what He laid out
in His Word. In college I gave away most of my clothes to
the homeless, felt guilty about owning any car, even a used
car, and did my best not to "love the world" by avoiding the
world altogether.

What we see in the Bible is that things like laughter, joy,
people, money, and food are all created by God to give pleasure. In Genesis, God crowns His creation of people, plants,
trees, and animals with the words it was "very good!" (1:31).
Even though we live in a broken world, we still experience
this good creation.

Some moments remind me of the simple goodness of God's
creation in undeniable ways. Recently, on a family vacation
we drove past some strawberry fields in California where you
could pick your own right off the farm. We stopped and
bought some and all I heard after this were oohs and ahhhs

from the minivan. The strawberries tasted so amazing! God invented that burst of pure strawberry sweetness.

Or have you ever walked in a forest after it snowed? The air is so clean and fresh and everything is totally silent. The trees are draped in white and the new snow crunches under your feet as you walk. You breathe in deep and watch your breath exhale in the cold air and think, *This is so beautiful.* God made all the details and made them to be very good.

Or maybe you remember a special moment of connection with someone, where you just felt so close, so accepted...so known. As you picture that person's arms wrapped around you, the feeling of love is just so incredible. This emanates from God and it's very, very good.

What's tragic, however, is that even though God is the inventor of pleasure, the average person has it in their mind that He's some kind of Cosmic Killjoy. They think He's this all-seeing, all-knowing traffic cop just looking for people who are enjoying themselves so He can bust them.

We view Him a lot like kids see their parents when their mom and dad put limits on them. I don't know what your kids are like, but mine would love to eat candy and watch TV all day. Throw in some Taco Bell and video games and they're golden. They don't like it when I place limits. Yet because I want my kids to turn into decent, competent, well-nourished human beings, I don't want them to get too much of what they perceive as a good thing. So I place limits on them, which are often challenged.

I'll walk in and say to my kids, "Okay, time to shut off the game, that's enough." And I hear the typical, "Come on, Dad, just one more game!"

I say, "Time to put the computer away and get ready for bed."

"Plllleeeeaassse, Dad, just one more hour!"

I'm asked, "Dad, can I have a cookie?" and as soon as the yes is out of my mouth, I hear, "Can I have two cookies?"

And when I say no, our kids look at me like I'm an ogre. They act like I'm the most restrictive, unfair prison warden that has ever parented a child. They sulk, whine, drag their feet, and at times they flat-out don't listen. They forget this very important truth: I bought them the game, gave them the cookies, and read them the bedtime book! I'm not the monster looking to minimize their pleasure; *I'm the one who brought it into their lives.* I want them to play, enjoy treats, and hear stories, but my primary concern isn't just their pleasure, but their development.

I know something their candy-fixated eyes can't see in that moment. The path they want to take, the path of cookies, candy, games, and never sleeping, doesn't lead to a place worth being. And that's the thing about pleasures: they are good and God created them and allows us to experience them. But when you pursue them over things that are more important—like your own health, your relationships, and your spiritual life—you end up stuck in a place you were never meant to be. A place that is unhealthy. A place that Solomon would tell you is meaningless.

PATHWAY TO PLEASURE

The problem with pleasure "under the sun" is that the more you experience it, the less it seems to satisfy. I mean, nothing says pleasure to me like Blue Bell Homemade Vanilla Ice Cream. This fantastic frozen bit of heaven is made in Texas and not yet available in Nevada, but a friend of mine recently sent me five gallons of Blue Bell packed in dry ice. (Now, that's a friend!) After a long weekend of church services, I'll come home on Sunday afternoon and reward myself with a huge Coke float. It is so good, but if I ever thought about having a second, I know it's just too rich. I can't stomach it. The more Coke floats, the less satisfaction.

Neuroscience has revealed similar findings with addiction. One example is that those who are addicted to drugs don't get a greater reward from getting high. As Dr. John Linden put it, "They actually seem to *want it more but like it less.*"[7] The drugs and addictive substances don't provide lasting satisfaction.

When our pathway to pleasure is blocked, we get frustrated because we believe if we just had more, we'd be happy. We think, if we just had additional money, then we could take that vacation or quit that job and then we would feel good. If we just had more free time, then we could pursue that hobby we don't have time for and do that project we always dreamed of. If our spouse would just agree, if our boss just wasn't a jerk, if the customers weren't so horrible, if our kids would just do what we ask the first time we ask, or if God didn't have those Ten Commandments, then we would finally find the pleasure we seek. We would finally feel good all the time.

But according to Solomon, who had all the time, money, and moral freedom to head farther down the road than any of us, these aren't the roadblocks: "So I decided there is nothing better than to enjoy food and drink and to find satisfaction in work. *Then I realized that these pleasures are from the hand of God* [italics added]. For who can eat or enjoy anything apart from him?" (Ecclesiastes 2:24–25).

Even Solomon coming out of his confused, backslid, far-from-God state realized that lasting pleasures are from God. They don't ultimately come from money, time, freedom, power, or influence, but from the hand of God. Without God, there is no ultimate good life.

When you seek pleasure for pleasure's sake, it's an ever-tightening spiral that leads to dissatisfaction. It's like my Coke floats; more doesn't make them better. But if you seek God, you find pleasure in simple things—an ever-widening, ever-growing world of simple joys and deep pleasures, sometimes where you least expect them.

One person lives a life of one-night stands but feels less and less satisfied and connected with each encounter. Another person commits to a God-honoring relationship, and finds pleasure in connection, intimacy, and trustworthy commitment.

One person lives for the weekends, blowing their entire paycheck on things they don't even remember the next morning. Another person gives their life, time, and resources to God each day and finds purpose, healing, and joy they will never forget.

One person escapes into a bottle, a video game, or their DVR and loses their life, one drink at a time, one level at a time, one hour at a time—pursuing a pleasure that is ever shrinking. Another does the hard work of facing their mistakes, reengaging their dreams, and sharing the love God has shared with them.

So we all have to ask ourselves, "Am I the person that's pursuing pleasure but feeling less and less? Or am I the person that's seeking God, wanting more of Him with the more I experience of Him?"

DANGER ZONE

Like any parent, God delights when His kids find joy in what He has created. Just because pleasure can lead to dangerous places doesn't mean we should be reactionary or avoid it altogether. The answer isn't to run away from all dancing, prohibit any form of sex, or deny oneself cheesecake, but to enjoy them in their proper context and don't expect more from them than they were created to give.

Sex is a gift created by God to be enjoyed within the context of marriage. Wine is mentioned often in the Bible, but drunkenness is a sin. Food is to be celebrated and enjoyed, but not at the expense of our health.

Pleasures must be held in check, but they shouldn't be avoided by Christians simply because they *might* lead to problems. Just about anything in our lives could lead to an addiction if we allowed it to. Food is awesome, but unchecked it can lead to obesity and all kinds of health challenges. Nothing feels better than a good night's sleep when you're tired, but if we lounge in bed every day, we can become lazy and waste our lives away. A drink can spice up a meal or conversation, but you can drink yourself into a gutter.

Work can be meaningful and engaging, but you can become a workaholic to the detriment of your family. Shopping can be a blast, but you can become preoccupied and over your head in debt. Prescription medications can help your body heal and help one cope with pain, but they can be abused and lead to destructive dependency. Sports are fun, but becoming obsessed with the Cubs can lead to ongoing depression (not that I would know—just sayin').

Pleasures are gifts that can be enjoyed under God, but any of them can be dangerous. I rarely drink alcohol, and on that rare occasion when I do, it is always with others in an appropriate social setting. Even when I wrestled with drug addiction, alcohol was never a temptation for me. But I have many friends who almost destroyed their lives because of alcohol. For them, they can't touch it, and I'm sensitive about anybody drinking around them.

My wife's grandfather was an alcoholic for many years and it deeply scarred their family. She grew up going to AA meetings with her grandfather and the only occasion they ever celebrated of her grandfather's was his sobriety day. Any form of alcohol was off-limits for him, but it doesn't mean that it is off-limits for everyone. Don't make your problem area everybody's problem area, and be respectful of their struggle.

Paul writes of the freedom we have in Christ. He says, "You say, 'I am allowed to do anything'—but not everything is good for you. And even though 'I am allowed to do anything,' I must not become a slave to anything" (1 Corinthians 6:12). He's quoting a statement that was used in the Christian community celebrating the freedom God brings to us in Christ. But this isn't a license to sin. Anything that controls us can become a problem.

Our bodies are much more than biological pleasure machines. We are spiritual beings and how we treat our bodies matters. Paul continues, "You say, 'Food was made for the stomach, and the stomach for food.' (This is true, though someday God will do away with both of them.) But you can't say that our bodies were made for sexual immorality. They were made for the Lord, and the Lord cares about our bodies" (1 Corinthians 6:13). We can't simply reduce sex to a physical act for physical pleasures; sex is also a spiritual act with spiritual consequences. We were made for God, and when we live for Him, we can enjoy the pleasures He provides. Sex, food, rest, and drink are good things, but we need wisdom and discernment not to distort them.

One of the greatest indicators that something's become a problem is when we begin to keep it a secret from those we love. When we start hiding credit cards, sneaking around with alcohol, slipping in extra doughnuts in spite of our high blood pressure, getting another prescription filled when we know we shouldn't. When we hide and refuse to reveal what is happening in our lives with those closest to us, this is a big red flag indicating we're longing for more than any drink, bite, or dose can provide. Bring it into the light with friends and with God. Face the sin because it threatens to steal so much of the good God wants to provide.

YEEEAAAHHH!

At two years old, my nephew Austin knew only one word—"yeah." He said it big, "Yeeeaaahhhh!" like the happiest little kid in the world. It was a blast to ask questions just to hear his response.

I'd say, "Austin, are the Dallas Cowboys the best football team ever?"

"Yeeeaaahhh!"

"Is it okay if I don't help Lori around the house today?"

"Yeeeaaahhh!"

"Should someone give me a foot massage?"

"Yeeeaaahhh!"

When Austin and his family stayed with us for a week, he and I got some time alone together in the living room one morning while everyone was getting ready. He was watching cartoons, and I thought it would be a perfect time to change the channel and put on a little Sports Center.

I forgot the number one rule of the toddler—don't mess with the TV when they are content. When I grabbed the remote control and switched the channel to ESPN, Austin looked confused for a minute and then looked at me like I was out of my mind. He looked back at the TV and back to me. He wasn't thinking, *Yeeeeaaaahhhh*. His whole body began to shake and his face turned red. He took a deep breath and prepared to scream at the top of his lungs at his completely out-of-touch and insensitive uncle.

I desperately looked around for something to diffuse the situation and saw a cupcake nearby. I held it out to him just as he was about to let it all out: "Austin—cupcake?" He got about a half second into his scream and it turned into "Yeeeaaahhh!" He reached out with both hands and was a happy camper again.

I don't know officially if Austin was old enough for cupcakes, but hey, you do what you have to do. We watched a little Sports Center and munched on the cupcake together, which was way better than morning cartoons anyway!

Austin reminds me of how what we focus on has a huge impact. We may derive loads of pleasure from some things, but eventually someone changes the channel or turns the TV off. The ultimate source of pleasure that lasts is found in God Himself and saying, "Yeeeaahhh" to Him. "Taste and see that the LORD is good. Oh, the joys of those who take refuge in him!" (Psalm 34:8). When we live toward Him, when we taste and see how good He is, we experience an enduring pleasure even through the ups and downs of life.

Every temporary pleasure finds a higher gratification when we direct our thanks to God. You enjoy a great meal, but as you direct your gratitude to God, that momentary pleasure becomes grounded in something so much greater. You enjoy a beautiful sunset, but rather than stopping there, you turn it into a moment of worship. You watch your kids sleep and re-member who entrusted them to you. Every small pleasure is an opportunity to thank the One who gave it and to say yes to God.

Knowing God and experiencing His goodness provide us with pleasure not just for the short term, but forever. David prayed: "You will show me the way of life, granting me the joy of your presence and the pleasures of living with you forever" (Psalm 17:11). When we say yes to God each moment, we live in His presence and there is joy. We were made for this joy, and we'll keep seeking it everywhere else until we find it in Him. God allows us to experience not only the joy of His presence today, but the pleasures of living with Him forever. The closer you get to God, the more you experience His pleasure.

Our closeness with Him will finally culminate in heaven someday. But the hope of heaven isn't just a blissed-out state of no more tears. The best part of heaven isn't that we'll see loved ones who have gone before us or that we'll receive new bodies. The best part of heaven is that God is there and we'll experience more of Him. We get to live in the pleasure of His company forever! God isn't the roadblock, but the pathway to lasting pleasure.

Chapter Three

Yes to Work

If it falls to your lot to be a street sweeper, sweep
the streets like Michelangelo painted pictures, like
Shakespeare wrote poetry, like Beethoven com-
posed music...

—Martin Luther King, Jr.

One summer I worked as a breakfast cook for the restaurant
chain Grandy's. For the uninitiated, Grandy's provides a fast-
food version of Cracker Barrel—down-home food to remind
you of Grandma's served speedy quick, at least that's the idea.
Without a doubt, Grandy's was the worst job I ever had. Not
because of the work or the company, but because my boss was
a real bummer.

She wore black tennis shoes with extra-thick soles and always tucked her well-ironed, tan Grandy's shirt in for good
measure. Her perfectly positioned name tag said it all: MARY,
MANAGER. I wanted to believe that "Mary, Mom" or "Mary,
Friend" was a nice person, but "Mary, Manager" was something else.

From the time I got off work until my alarm went off

at 3:15 a.m. the next morning, I dreaded seeing Mary. My responsibilities included being at work by 4 a.m. to start making the gravy for the day. As "Mary, Manager" always reminded me, there was only one opportunity a day to make the huge bin of gravy. If it wasn't right, there was no time to fix it in the breakfast rush. The fate of everyone's gravy experience at Grandy's rested on *my* shoulders. And as Mary was quick to testify, I had ruined some customers' mornings more than once.

If you've ever seen the character from *Seinfeld* known as the Soup Nazi, then you'll understand what I mean when I say Mary was the Gravy Nazi. Every morning she would come in after I had made a huge tub of gravy, calling me in to be there with her for the tasting. Slowly she would put her spoon in the gravy, sniff like a wine connoisseur, raise it to her lips, and taste it. Every now and then she'd shrug and say, "Passable," but most days she would throw a wall-eyed hissy fit and berate me until I felt smaller than a cockroach. "And you call yourself a gravy cook?" Well, actually I'm not sure that's something I'd ever put on my résumé.

After my verbal lashing, Mary would leave and I'd walk over and try out the "horrible" gravy, which always tasted the same to me. After all, I followed the same recipe and measured out all the ingredients exactly as Grandma Grandy called for. I mean, I was losing sleep over this gravy! Then I finally realized her response to the gravy was more about her mood that morning than it was about the gravy. Needless to say, I was so relieved the day I got another job and put in my notice. Even now I can't look at a bowl of gravy without getting a little queasy.

PUBLIC WORKS

Whether you've ever worked for a Gravy Nazi or not, we all relate to the struggle with work. Maybe you just wish you could get out from under an oppressive boss or tedious busywork. Perhaps you thought your job would be a dream, but the endless hours, problems, and conflicts wear you down and demand more and more—suddenly, it's not so dreamy anymore. Maybe you feel like you chose the wrong career and wish you had the courage to switch jobs. Many people dream about quitting their present employer and starting their own business. But even those fortunate enough to consider themselves entrepreneurs still struggle with work.

Most people don't have their dream jobs and feel lucky to have a job at all, even if they don't feel so lucky driving into work. According to a 2009 study, 55 percent of Americans, more than half, are not satisfied with their jobs. This is the lowest that number has been in twenty-two years.[8] We may live in better houses and have nicer stuff, but the constant consumerism hasn't provided many of us with more fulfilling, less stressful lives.

Think for a moment. On a scale of 1 to 10, how much do you enjoy your present job? When you think about the parts of your life you love the most, does work ever cross your mind? We may even wonder, is it possible to work and be happy? Can we ever enjoy what we do to earn a living?

If anybody had his or her dream job, it would be Solomon. He ruled in peacetime, meaning there were no wars to fight, so trade was permitted with other nations. His country was growing and rule was secure. Everything he did turned to gold. Solomon threw himself into work. He built incredible structures, owned vineyards that produced the best wine, struck business deals, navigated agreements for trade with other nations, and became filthy rich. He "made silver as plentiful in Jerusalem as stone" (1 Kings 10:27). There were no brutal morning commutes, no worries about things like insurance and retirement plans. He wasn't working "for the man"; he *was* the man.

Late in his life he entered the phase where he could fully enjoy all his accomplishments. He could put his feet up and take in the rewards of all his labor. Yet he looked back at all his achievements and said: "I came to hate all my hard work here on earth, for I must leave to others everything I have earned. And who can tell whether my successors will be wise or foolish? Yet they will control everything I have gained by my skill and hard work under the sun. How meaningless! So I gave up in despair, questioning the value of all my hard work in this world" (Ecclesiastes 2:18–20).

So many people are in similar emotional places, having given up on work in despair. They are simply biding their time, clocking in and clocking out, waiting for the workday to be over. Solomon was particularly bothered by the fact that all his wealth would go to others after him, people who might squander it foolishly.

In fact, his fears were well founded. Solomon did end up leaving his wealth to his son Rehoboam, who lost ten-twelfths of the kingdom Solomon had firmly established with so much work (1 Kings 12). Solomon seems to have engaged in work merely as a means to gain and to feel good about himself. In the end, all of it added up to chasing after the wind. How's that for a retirement wake-up call?

WORKING FOR THE WEEKEND

There is another way to consider our life's work. When we say yes to God, it impacts all of our lives, especially how we view work. Many of us miss a level of satisfaction we can experience at work because we rarely see work as a spiritual act. Yet when we invite God into our work, it can begin to transform our experience. It may still be hard, we may still pray and plan to get into a different career, but God can bring meaning to us even in the everyday tasks we perform.

We've all heard or said the phrase "I'm working for the weekend." Often this statement implies that work itself is the problem, and without a doubt, it requires effort and consumes energy. But work is a good thing God created. When you consider that we spend one-third of our lives working and another third sleeping, you realize how critical it is that we think about and like our work. We may have the same old job, but through faith we can have a brand-new occupation.

In the very first pages of the Bible, we read that on "the seventh day God had finished his *work* of creation, so he rested from all his *work*" (Genesis 2:2). God is a God who works. Many of the images of God throughout the Bible are images of a worker. He is described as a composer, performer, metalworker, potter, garment maker, gardener, farmer, shepherd, tentmaker, and builder.[9]

The image of God presented in the first pages of Genesis is consumed with work. He creates, He brings forth, He labors and works, and then, on the seventh day, He rests from His work. All of these roles and endeavors remind us of the importance of work to God. If God works, then it must be good.

As we're created in His image, God also created us to work. After God creates people in Genesis, he plants a garden and "placed the man in the Garden of Eden to tend and watch over it" (Genesis 2:15). There are a lot of jokes out there about the world's oldest profession, but it turns out the world's first job was a gardener. As soon as humans were created, work was created, too, because when we work—when we tend things, make things, watch over things—we're being like our Creator.

In the creation account of Genesis, we read twice that humans are to have "dominion" over the earth (Genesis 1:28). We are to rule the fish of the sea and the birds of the air. Christian author Andy Crouch notes how remarkable it is that the "biblical author who had seen neither airplanes, nor submarines, and for whom boats were small and rudimentary affairs, could anticipate humankind being able to 'rule' over fish and birds in a meaningful way."[10] Yet God foreshadowed events over the next thousand years and communicated His intent for us to be responsible in managing all of His creation.

Later on in Genesis after Adam and Eve eat from the forbidden tree of the knowledge of good and evil, we have the first firing (long before Donald Trump) when God throws them out of the garden. A lot of people think this is where God cursed work, but when you read the text, God curses the *ground*, meaning that work will take more effort, not work itself. God says: "All your life you will struggle to scratch a living from it [the ground]" (Genesis 3:17). Work is a blessing now filled with difficulties, struggle, and toil to survive, but it is still a gift.

We were made to work. Consider retired people—most of the ones I know are some of the busiest people I know! They don't get paid, but they work. My dad used to love to pick up stereo equipment at garage sales. One whole closet in a spare bedroom was filled with tape decks hooked up to record players, hooked up to a CD player, hooked up to an 8-track. When his friends needed an old record transferred to a tape, or an old 8-track burned to a CD, my dad did it for them. He'd string wires and press buttons on all this used, ancient gear, and he would straight up crank the stuff out. He loved doing it!

My dad was doing what was fun for him, but he was still working. He was always busy either making tapes or helping someone fix their house or serving a nonprofit with work around their building. He understood we weren't made to just sit around. When people retire and they stop getting out and doing things, it quickly affects their health and emotional well-being. We weren't just made to work; we *need* to work. Without it, we lose a sense of our purpose and identity, a sense of what we're here on earth to accomplish.

When my kids play together, especially when they just use their imaginations and set up stuffed animal worlds, sometimes I listen in on their conversation, and guess what, it's always about work. They're setting up houses and roads and stores and rules and making stuff. They are overseeing and tending. They're playing at working.

When we bring order out of chaos or put something good

or beautiful in the world, when we help people who need it, or use any of our gifts to serve others, God is delighted. Even in heaven I believe we will have meaningful work to do. When it comes to our satisfaction with life and with our jobs, work is not the problem.

OCCUPATIONAL HAZARD

We see all kinds of workers in the Bible interacting with God, being used by Him, and worshipping Him: farmers, shepherds, musicians, artists, metalworkers, politicians, military leaders, government workers, tent makers, stay-at-home moms, fishermen, carpenters, seamstresses, jailers, tax people, innkeepers, and retail workers. In fact, biblical scholar Paul Minear writes that the Bible is "an album of casual photographs of laborers....A book by workers, about workers, for workers."[11] Most of these workers are not in directly religious types of jobs. They were doing all kinds of work in their culture, from great leadership tasks to the smallest acts of daily labor. Yet their work was not separated from their faith.

This is seen all the way back in Genesis when humankind was called to "cultivate" the earth (2:15). In the original language the term "cultivate" is also translated as "work," "service," "craftsmanship" and surprisingly in some contexts, "worship." The term is used to describe the work the Israelites did of making bricks and working in the fields while in slavery under Egypt (Exodus 1:14), the craftsmen who worked on the temple (Exodus 35:24), and those who made fine linen (1 Chronicles 4:21). Solomon uses the term when he assigned the Levites and priests to lead the people in worship (2

Chronicles 8:14). Though the word has its own distinct nu-
ances, there is an interconnected link between work, service,
and worship. Whether we are working as a seamstress, laying
brick at a construction site, or leading people in a church service—it is all work and it is all worship![12]

Today, however, we like to put things in categories of secular and sacred. We have secular and sacred music, buildings,
spaces, and work. With this view we start to see our lives more
like waffles with little squares that separate our work life, our
church life, our romantic life, our kids' lives, and so on. Jesus
calls for us to live a more integrated life, more like spaghetti
noodles, all in the same pot and wrapped around each other.

God is not one of the cubes in a waffle, but instead He is
the actual wheat that all the noodles are made of. He is not a
piece of your life, but rather the very ingredient of every piece
of our tangled lives. He's calling us to see all of our life as spiritual. We don't just have family time, church time, and work
time; it is all *God time*.

The amazing news is we can go to the same old job, but
we can have a whole new occupation. Paul challenges us in
the Bible: "Work willingly at whatever you do, as though you
were working for the Lord rather than for people" (Colossians
3:23).

Think about your job title for a moment.

You're not just a waitress; you're a waitress *for the Lord*.

You're not just a bellman; you're a bellman *for the Lord*.

You're not just a regional director of sales; you're a regional
director of sales *for the Lord*.

You're not just a stay-at-home mom; you're a stay-at-home
mom *for the Lord*.

You're not just a retail associate; you're a retail associate *for the Lord.*

You're not just a teacher; you're a teacher *for the Lord.*

You're not just a pipe fitter; you're a pipe fitter *for the Lord.*

You're not just a police officer; you're a police officer *for the Lord.*

Everything takes on new meaning when we do it for the Lord. Paul restates the idea this way: "So whether you eat or drink, or whatever you do, do it all for the glory of God" (1 Corinthians 10:31). The "whatever you do" includes laundry and dirty dishes, mopping up the floor, and mowing the yard. We have to do these tasks anyway, so why not do them with an awareness that we work for God? In that act there is more opportunity for gratitude, for joy, and for thanksgiving as we direct our hearts beyond the stress of work to the God who created it as a blessing.

Now I'm sure some of you are reading this and thinking, "Okay, so working as if for the Lord sounds nice, but you don't know my boss. You don't know my coworkers. They're horrible. And stuff I have to do—it just doesn't excite me at all. It's a dark place. God isn't a part of the deal."

Maybe you're not just at work to get a paycheck, but for a mission. God may be hard to see in your job, but He's part of you. And so long as you're there, He's there. It may be a dark place, but God's light can shine through you. If your job doesn't fire you up, you can fire up your job with a new occupation. I'm not talking about carrying your Bible around, using lots of spiritual-sounding language, or trying to force people to sing gospel songs in the break room. From the outside, things may appear the same, but internally you see things differently. It's as simple as this: right before you head into work each day, pray, "God, I'm going to my job, but I'm serving You. Help me do my work well, for You."

A few words, a couple sentences, a moment of reflection on what you are doing and the impact is exponential. Pray before you boot up your computer or start e-mailing. Pray before you clock in or before you start to mix the gravy, even if it is 4 a.m.! If we went to work tomorrow with new occupations, imagine what God could do. Imagine how our attitudes would change. How our work would improve. The daily tasks we did yesterday would be filled with more meaning today!

DREAM JOB

A new occupation mentality will serve us well in our current job, but shouldn't hold us back from also pursuing work that we feel we were created to do. What are the dreams God has placed in your heart? What is the big dream you would go after if money were no object? What is the work you most enjoy doing?

The only way to get there is to begin small today. As business and marketing expert Seth Godin wrote: "We need to stop shopping for lightning bolts. You don't win an Olympic gold medal with a few weeks of intensive training. There's no such thing as an overnight opera sensation. Great law firms or design companies don't spring up overnight.... Every great company, every great brand, and every great career has been built in exactly the same way: bit by bit, step by step, little by little."[13] He's right. Tomorrow's possibility is determined by today's hard work. There are no shortcuts.

Paul wrote to Timothy: "Work hard so you can present yourself to God and receive his approval" (2 Timothy 2:15). The phrase "work hard" carries the idea of having a passionate determination to accomplish a particular goal. We are to give maximum effort to the dreams and goals God has put inside us. Timothy was called to be a pastor and teacher. He was to have an unreserved commitment to do his best in examining, interpreting, explaining, and applying the Bible.

Sometimes we think we'll reach our dream job by luck or by some opportunity. We think that if only my boss would give me a break, if only I got that raise, if only I had the start-up money, and if only I had the right situation. But Paul says, "Be a good worker, one who does not need to be ashamed and who correctly explains the word of truth" (2 Timothy 2:15). The expression "correctly explains" comes from a term that means "to cut straight." It was used of a craftsman making a straight cut, of a farmer plowing a straight row, of a mason setting a straight line of bricks, or of workers building a straight road. It represents the careful performing of any task. If we are going to carefully explain the Bible, or correctly pursue a career God has put in our heart, we'll have to cut a straight path to help us get there.

WORKING OVER TIME

It's not easy seeing how to make the leap from where you are now to where you'd like to be working in the future. Toward that goal, here are some questions to consider in cutting the path toward your dream job:

1. What are my goals?

A friend of mine is a professional golfer on the LPGA tour. She says she got there by not only having natural talent, but also having daily goals, weekly goals, monthly goals, and yearly goals. All of them are directed at the big dream she feels God led her to pursue. She keeps them posted on her wall so she can see them visually. And she loves the process of achieving these goals, which include diet, workout regimen, training schedule, and *lots* of golf. The most important aspect of her goals is that she has small, achievable goals building toward a larger goal.

If you want to go back to college for another career, you need to plan out how that could happen and set goals that are attainable on the way to the big goal. You may not know all of what is involved, but you can start small. For example, if you've always dreamed of working in the medical field and helping people physically, start with trying to find someone in that profession and take him or her out to lunch. Learn more about what the profession is really like—the good and the bad.

Set a goal to read a couple books about what is involved in that occupation. You don't have to figure it all out, but set clear, attainable goals to move the ball down the field. Goals move a dream into reality, and what we do every day sets the course of our lives. Don't get paralyzed by a massive dream; write down some achievable goals today.

2. What am I doing today to prepare for tomorrow's opportunity?

People who are just waiting for the big break won't be ready when it comes. I felt called to encourage people with written words and help them live out their faith more fully so I began writing. I didn't have a book contract. I couldn't get anyone other than friends and family to read my stuff, but this didn't hinder me. I wrote my first book without a contract, self-published it, and sold it on my own.

I loved the process of writing so I wrote another book by dedicating an hour a day most days, early in the morning, to writing. I still couldn't land a book contract, but I kept writing and trying to get better. One day a guy I hardly knew came up to me and said, "Jud, my friend is the president of a major publishing company. I'm going to send your self-published book to him, to show him what you've done. Do you have anything else I could pass on to him?" I hardly knew this man. I didn't know he was a retired counselor, professor, and author who had books in multiple languages published around the world that had been in print for over twenty-five years.

Literally that morning, only two hours before, I had finished a complete draft to my second book. I said, "Give me five minutes," and I walked to my computer and hit print. He took the manuscript and mailed it to his friend, the publishing president. He also encouraged me to send in a proposal through the regular route. He sent the manuscript in and I mailed my unsolicited proposal to the publisher and waited.

A couple months later the publisher called and said that

the president had looked at my manuscript and they were ready to publish it as it was. I was thrilled to say the least. What cracked me up is that within the next couple days, I also got an official rejection letter from the same publisher for the book proposal I'd mailed in through the normal channels. You could say that I just got a break, that things just fell together for me, that God opened the door. All of that is true, but don't miss this—none of this would have been possible if I had waited around for a publisher without having a manuscript ready to go. After all, they accepted the whole book but rejected my proposal! I felt called to write and so I gave myself to the task and loved the work little by little, step by step.

Everyone who achieves a dream started pursuing it when *no one was watching* and *no one was paying them* to do it. If you love doing something, then what are you waiting for? Go for it. If you feel led to teach, start taking a class or getting your credentials, even if it means taking one class at a time. If you have a dream to act, start taking lessons or join a community theater. If you have a dream to write, start writing. Don't wait for the big dream to just drop in your lap. Don't wait to get paid for your dream. Start living the dream today. Do what you love and do it so well that eventually people will pay you for it.

3. Can I love the work more than the recognition?

If you followed the most highly successful people around, you'd be surprised at how boring and routine their daily lives are. A highly successful athlete gives most of his or her time to training and preparing for the game. A writer spends much of his or her life in front of a computer screen. A director spends all his or her time in the monotonous details of making movies.

Sometimes we look at others' achievements and think that is what we want—the reward from the work. We see ourselves winning an Oscar or a Nobel Prize or a Grammy or a Pulitzer. But recognition is not enough if you don't love the work. We've got to fall in love with the process, the hard work, of going after our dream, or we'll be miserable if we happen to achieve it. What drives a person who sustains a long career is a love of the process and the work. The award is just the result of all that work. And more recognition just leads to doing more of the same work!

If you start teaching or taking lessons or trying to work yourself out of your current job and you don't enjoy the process, find another area to focus on that you do enjoy. Success would only mean that you have to give more of yourself to something you don't really enjoy doing.

Start now to "present yourself to God and receive his approval" (2 Timothy 2:15). Paul used the term "present" that literally means "to stand alongside, to present oneself for inspection." We are to manage the gifts, dreams, and passions God has given us and present ourselves to God as one approved.

CONFESSIONS OF A WORKAHOLIC

No matter how much you enjoy your work, it must never become an idol or a substitute for God. I learned this the hard way. After I finished school and became a pastor, I entered into a phase of my life where I began to make work the main thing. The church where I came to faith and later served as a pastor had a strong work ethic. The building that we met in had a plaque out front that said, TO THE GLORY OF GOD BY A PEOPLE WITH A MIND TO WORK.

I keyed in on the last part of that sentence and went about working with all my heart. I was doing things that I loved, teaching people about the Bible, visiting people in the hospital, helping people work through difficulties, celebrating people's marriages and baptisms, providing leadership to volunteer teams. This was a large church and staff, and I prided myself on how often I was the first person in the office in the morning, turning the alarm off as I arrived. I took joy in setting the alarm at night when I was the last person to leave. But somewhere in all of this busyness, I began to make my work more like a substitute for my relationship with God.

Later, when I got married and we had children and moved to another city, I began to pay the price for making something other than God Himself the center of my life. Finally, I began to realize something had gone very wrong: I overheard my wife say to a friend on the phone one night that she felt like a single mom because I was always gone, either physically or emotionally. Then another time my six-year-old daughter said, "Dad, I wish you weren't a pastor," as I was heading out the door to help yet another person in crisis. My own family suffered as my primary relationship—with them and with God—became eclipsed by my dedication to being the perfect pastor.

And there was a physical cost to pay as well. One night after giving a message, I was walking up the stairs going back to my office when my legs gave out and I collapsed. I couldn't move and couldn't catch my breath. I don't know how long I was out of it, but eventually someone came and helped me get somewhere and lie down. As she was virtually carrying me to the couch, this staff member said, "We've been taking bets on when this would happen. You can only do so much before you pay a price." Message received loud and clear—I've never forgotten her words since.

In the end it was just my body sending a warning shot. If I kept going at my current pace, then the toll was going to destroy me. But for me this physical warning was more than just working a lot. I had made my job more like my God. Any job, even a ministry job, is a bad god and bad gods consume you. They demand all you give them, and they require human sacrifice.

LIFE-WORK BALANCING ACT

Solomon's memoir has been called the confessions of a workaholic. He made work number one and it failed him. He continued his observations: "So what do people get in this life for all their hard work and anxiety? Their days of labor are filled with pain and grief; even at night their minds cannot rest. It is all meaningless" (Ecclesiastes 2:22–23). He says work is a vexation. Our minds always worrying, the pressures of clients and tasks, the worries about layoffs and cutbacks and profit margins. Will I be able to keep my job? Will my company survive? Will I ever be able to retire? Will I ever be able to enjoy life?

Solomon describes someone without child or brother who

works so hard and then one day wakes up and realizes, "Who am I working for? Why am I giving up so much pleasure now?" (Ecclesiastes 4:8). When work becomes your God, your whole life swings out of balance. Those of us who thrive on achievement tend to get a lot of self-worth from what we do. We love to exceed expectations, enjoy the thrill of the sale or delivering on time. The praise of our coworkers and leaders fires us up. Earning promotions can begin to consume us. All this stuff is good, but if we make them the ultimate thing, we begin to suffer the consequences. Our relationships wither. Our health starts to decline. We get more and more distant from God, and then one day we look up, and just like Solomon mentioned, we realize how much we have lost.

The safeguard God put into our lives with work is the Sabbath. We read that God worked and He rested in Genesis. He didn't rest because He was worn out; He's God! He rested as a sign of His rule and to empower us to follow His example. In the Ten Commandments, God said, "You have six days each week for your ordinary work, but the seventh day is a Sabbath day of rest dedicated to the Lord your God. On that day no one in your household may do any work" (Exodus 20:9–10).

God set up a rhythm to life. We should work hard and rest hard, cultivate passionately and rest equally as passionately. The New Testament teaches that the Sabbath is no longer a literal Saturday, but a whole era: "There remains, then, a Sabbath-rest for the people of God; for anyone who enters God's rest also rests from his own work, just as God did from his" (Hebrews 4:9–10). We rest in God each day through faith and trust. Yet the principle of a day of rest each week is hardwired into creation. When we ignore the principle, we pay a price.

I've found I am more effective with a full day of rest than working seven days straight. Sometimes it takes a heroic effort to pull off a full day away from work, but do it anyway. You can leave projects unfinished and e-mails unanswered. They're still going to be there when you return.

Make it a priority to identify things that fill you up when we feel emotionally, physically, or spiritually tired. The Sabbath was all about devotion to God, but sometimes reconnecting with God may come through unconventional means. Everybody is different, and finding your path to growing in your faith is essential. Part of a day of rest can also just be fun! Taking in a baseball game while devouring nachos may do a lot for you, or working in the garden. Reading a book can fill your mind with new ideas. Maybe you find solace in going to a concert, or on a five-mile run. Sometimes these activities of unwinding help us reconnect with a different perspective on our life and our faith.

The key to all of this is that we have to become okay with disappointing other people. We can't be all things to all people. But we can prioritize God, our family, and our friendships, and become more concerned about not disappointing *them*.

We have to be very in touch with how much we can process or take. Listen to your body, mind, friends, and family and get plenty of sleep—which is one of the simplest and most neglected practices we can engage in to avoid burnout.

Maybe your own health plan—starting today, for the long haul—is a good idea for you. You could start by asking questions about how much you work and who pays the price for your commitment. Do your friends and family ever see you? Have you made work more than God intended it to be? Is your pace sustainable for the long haul? Make a list of the top five people in your life. Find out how those individuals feel. God and people are what matter most in our lives, so prioritize time for them.

Even Solomon experiences a change of heart and attitude as he journeys back to God from the long detour. He says, "So I decided there is nothing better than to enjoy food and drink and to find satisfaction in work. Then I realized that these pleasures are from the hand of God" (Ecclesiastes 2:24). Here we see the possibility of finding satisfaction in work. More than gifting, promotions, spreadsheets, or the celebration of deals done and good work accomplished, satisfaction comes from God. When we work for Him, toward Him, and direct our thanks to Him for each work opportunity, we can be renewed.

Chapter Four

Yes to Seasons

In the depth of winter, I finally learned that
within me there lay an invincible summer.

—*Albert Camus*

A *gray* hair was growing out of my nose.

I stared in the mirror in shock. Only a few moments earlier, Lori and I were in the car backing out of our driveway when she said, "Jud, you have a long nose hair." I chuckled and kept on going, trying to make light of it. As lovingly as possible she said, "No, you don't understand. You have a gray hair sticking out of your nose and it is a *quarter inch long*. You need to trim it. *Now*."

One look at her and I knew she was serious. I pulled back into the driveway and went inside to take a look. I acted frustrated at the inconvenience, but I was mostly concerned. Gray hair coming out of my nose. *Really?*

Sure enough, there was this massive silver thread extending from my nostril like some bizarre overnight mutation or alien antenna. In that moment I thought of the elderly men I've known who often have hair growing out of their ears or nose. I used to think it was because they didn't care, but then I realized it's because these hairs sprout up overnight and those guys just haven't noticed yet! After tweezers took care of my problem, I went back out to the car and Lori and I laughed so hard we could barely pull it back together. (And yes, I begged her not to "tweet the tweeze" moment.)

PRESENT IN THE PRESENT

Despite making light of it, I began to see I was entering into a new season. One I wasn't sure I was particularly excited about welcoming. I was also reminded that life comes at us in seasons. One day you have a full head of hair; the next day it's thinning on top and growing in your ears. The seasons change and we're usually looking forward to the next one, wanting to skip time or rewind time, but rarely fully living in the season we're in right now.

When you are in middle school, you can't wait to be in high school. You get to high school and you can't wait to be in college. As soon as you hit college, you grow tired of class and want to be in the workforce to earn some cash. In the workforce you wish you were older, so that people would respect you more. Then you wake up with gray hair growing out of your nose and wish you were younger!

Single? You may want to be married. Married? You may wish you were single. Parents love their kids but also look forward to when their kids grow up so that the house will be quiet again. When the kids move on, you wish they would have some grandkids so things won't be so quiet!

It's the "next thing" syndrome. We get so fed up with the many challenges of the season we're in that we miss all the good there is to experience right now. If we aren't careful, we live our whole life waiting on the next season, and remembering the good ol' days, never fully present in the present.

Every season has its challenges. One of my dad's favorite sayings later in life was, "This, too, shall pass." And he knew what he was talking about. He'd lived through the Great Depression, served in World War II, and parented during the radical sixties. He owned a business through the recession of the seventies, and navigated the lives of four kids, including me. For more than eighty years he experienced the seasons of life—war and peace, prosperity and hard times, joy and sadness, great gain, and great loss. So he could say with authority, "This, too, shall pass so just hang in there." He had learned that life doesn't come at us as one long constant. It comes in seasons and there's a purpose for each one.

We've seen how saying yes to God opens our lives to enjoy Him and all the pleasures that He provides. We find satisfaction in work as we invite God into the daily tasks of life. Saying yes to God also means embracing the season that we're in and fully enjoying it. We learn to celebrate the good in life each day and be truly thankful.

TURN, TURN, TURN

Long before the Byrds immortalized His truth in their iconic song "Turn, Turn, Turn," Solomon described the variety of life's seasons in the most famous lines from Ecclesiastes:

*For everything there is a season, a time for every activity
under heaven.*
A time to be born and a time to die.
A time to plant and a time to harvest.
A time to kill and a time to heal.
A time to tear down and a time to build up.
A time to cry and a time to laugh.
A time to grieve and a time to dance.
A time to scatter stones and a time to gather stones.
A time to embrace and a time to turn away.
A time to search and a time to quit searching.
A time to keep and a time to throw away.
A time to tear and a time to mend.
A time to be quiet and a time to speak.
A time to love and a time to hate.
A time for war and a time for peace....
God has made everything beautiful for its own time.

(Ecclesiastes 3:1–8, 11)

As far as pop songs go, Solomon may be a one-hit wonder, but the timeless truth of his observation resonates today as much as it did when he wrote it. He uses a literary device known as *merismus*, which is defined as "the statement of polar extremes as a way of embracing everything that lies between them."[14] The list of opposites in this passage contains twenty-eight items in fourteen pairs—multiples of seven. Over the course of all his years, Solomon shrewdly noted that there's a time and place for all kinds of human actions and emotions. Long before postmodernists put such an emphasis on context, he knew that different life seasons require different responses.

Solomon wasn't the only one in Scripture to point out the importance of seasons. They're one of the major images of stability found in the Bible, and they point to regularity and wholeness. They order our world and lives. The Psalmist writes of God:

> *You made the moon to mark the seasons, and the sun knows when to set. You send the darkness, and it becomes night, when all the forest animals prowl about. Then the young lions roar for their prey, stalking the food provided by God. At dawn they slink back into their dens to rest. Then people go off to their work, where they labor until evening…*
>
>   (Psalm 104:19–23)

God has handcrafted the seasons and He rules over the rhythms of life. Seasons give us reprieve from monotony and show us hidden beauty we have not seen before. They allow for a change in place and a change in pace. They remind us of the movement of time. We often fight desperately against this movement, against the limitations of time. We schedule it, "manage" it, manipulate it, and try to squeeze more out of it. We deny it, run from it, and seek to beat it. We try to reverse the effects of time (including gray nose hairs!) with creams, pills, nips, and tucks, but these seasons are a gift and there is a "time for everything."

Seasons remind us that we are not in control. So many heroes of the faith lived through changing seasons in their lives: David goes from being a shepherd, to hiding in the caves on the run from King Saul, to being King himself, and then becoming a husband and father; Moses goes from a royal son, to a runaway in the desert, to a leader of people; Joseph goes from a favorite son, to a slave, to a prisoner, to an administrator and ruler; Jesus goes from a carpenter, to the desert, to his public ministry, to crucifixion, resurrection, and ascension. In all seasons, at all times, God was in control of their lives, just as He is in control of ours today.

WEATHER FORECAST

Have you ever noticed how much our seasons of the year are tied to weather? If it's summer, we complain about how hot it is. If it's winter, then it's too cold—and everything in between during spring and fall. We use the weather and the annual seasonal events to shape our expectations.

However, for all our modern technology—numerous satellites and Doppler radar and thermal imaging—people still cannot control the weather. I really like the fact that only God is powerful enough to direct the waves and the breezes, the clouds and the sunshine. We can predict and forecast and anticipate and expect all we want, but ultimately, He's the only One who knows.

When the weather is good, we enjoy it. Nothing can lift the spirits like a beautiful day. A day when there's no wind ripping off the car door when we open it. We roll the windows down, turn up some tunes, and slip our hand outside the window to feel the breeze. We take our lunch outside at work to soak up the sun or wash all the dirt and dead spiders off the patio furniture that once looked so new, and now looks like it's been exposed to nuclear fallout. We sit outside and enjoy it. We bask in it. It's a good day.

And what do we say to our kids when it's 11 a.m. and they're still in their pajamas in front of the TV on a day like that? "GO OUTSIDE!" Because days like that are special and they don't last forever. Pretty soon it will be too hot, cold, windy, or rainy. Enjoy the weather!

Sometimes I wonder if God wants to say the same to us. We take the good seasons for granted. We think every season will be like this; every day *should* be like this. We remain stuck inside ourselves, not even realizing the incredible gifts we have right in front of us. When you are in a time in your life where you don't have a lot of commitments pulling on you, don't let it slip through your fingers by stressing about the small stuff.

If you don't have some kind of chronic pain or discomfort, take it from those that are in that season right now that every pain-free day is a *massive* gift. Celebrate it! You may be in a season of raising kids, and there are certainly lots of challenges that come with that season, but it is also a gift. Children are a gift that many people wish they could have, a gift that empty nesters miss to the point of pressuring their adult kids to hurry up and give them grandchildren. When it's a good season, get out there and enjoy the weather, because difficult seasons will come.

HOT POTATO

Worrying is one of the biggest areas that keeps us from enjoying the season. I saw this in my kids when we recently had a big cleanup around our house. Our kids had to go through their toys, and we bagged some up to give to others. And even though they each stacked several things to give away, we still had to address the stuffed animal issue. My kids had collected so many stuffed animals and Wonder Pets of every size and variety over the years that it just became *ridiculous*. Purple hippos and pink elephants, lifelike puppies, and too-cute teddies—there were stuffed animals everywhere, under their beds, in their closets, in the corners of their rooms.

So we called a family meeting and told them they were each limited to . . . *thirty-five* stuffed animals apiece. (I assure you this was a full twenty stuffed animals more than I thought they'd ever need or actually play with.) Can you say "hoarders"?

They acted like we were crazy parents, and it would just be impossible to only own thirty-five stuffed animals. You would have thought we were asking them to give up their children or live animals that were family pets. As they were sorting through the animals, I could see the questions floating in the back of their minds centered on the idea of how much is *enough*. "Will there be enough stuffed animals if I get scared? Will there be enough stuffed animals if we're going on a road trip? Will there be enough stuffed animals if something happens and I can't get any more?"

We're not so different from my kids with their stuffed animals. We often allow the good seasons of life to be clouded by worry, especially worrying about having *enough*. Even in wonderful seasons we stress over thoughts like: Will there be enough in my retirement? Will there be enough time? Will there be enough good health? Is there enough house, cars, or clothes? In all our worry, we miss the good moments.

Jesus said, "That is why I tell you not to worry about everyday life—whether you have *enough* food to eat or enough clothes to wear" (Luke 12:22). Jesus is telling us not to place so much emphasis on *enough*. If Jesus told those who had but one simple garment not to worry about their clothing, what would He say to us with closets full of clothes and freezers full of food? God is the only place we will ever find enough, the only One who can satisfy our deepest longings.

Worry is taking responsibility for something God never intended for us to take responsibility for. It robs us of enjoying the season that we're in *now*. As Jesus so memorably put it, "Can all your worries add a single moment to your life? And if worry can't accomplish a little thing like that, what's the use of worrying over bigger things?" (Luke 12:25–26). All of our worry about our mortgage makes absolutely no difference to our mortgage. All of our worry about the banks, our job, finances, health, stuff, bills, and debt does not change any of it positively.

So how do we handle worry when it is robbing us of enjoying the season? We play "hot potato." Did you ever sit in a circle and play that game as a kid? Somebody throws the hot potato (usually an object that's not hot at all) and it lands in your lap. What do you do? Get rid of it! Throw it! You don't hold on to the hot potato. You toss it! When worry lands in our lap, we should treat it like a hot potato. We get rid of it by quickly tossing it to God. "Give all your worries and cares to God, for he cares about you" (1 Peter 5:7).

If you're like me, this works for a moment, at least a couple minutes, and then the hot potato comes back into your lap. You start worrying again, sometimes without even realizing it. So again, we give it to God. The secret is playing hot potato with our worries until it becomes a *habit*. Every time the worry comes, give it to God in prayer. Refuse to carry it. Admit we aren't in control, and focus on doing the things that we can do to change the situation. Over time we can *learn* how to face the worries of life by constantly casting those worries back in God's lap. Don't sit with a hot potato on your own.

SPOILER ALERT

Another thing that robs us of good seasons is complaining, which spoils so many good things in our lives. Lori recently took up a twenty-one-day challenge where she wore a bracelet, and every time she complained about anything, she moved it over to her other wrist. I didn't realize she was doing it, but I immediately noticed the change in her attitude. When she told me what she was doing, I thought it was really cool. Of course, I also took the liberty several times to say, "I think based on what you just said, you need to move that bracelet from one wrist over to the other." I had more fun with it than she did!

Lori inspired me to take up the no-complaint twenty-one-day challenge, without the bracelet. I think of myself as a positive person, but within the first day I was blown away at my complaints. I grumbled about things like the weather, the alarm going off too early, having to iron a shirt, waiting in line for, well, anything. It was ridiculous how many things I complained about that didn't matter. What I've noticed is how different my attitude is when I keep my complaining in check. Everything began to seem better. All my little inconveniences in life didn't seem so big.

Like worry, complaining doesn't change anything other than keep us pulled down in a negative cycle. Complaining is like scratching your arm when it's been in contact with poison ivy; it may bring some immediate relief, but it makes the situation worse in the end.

Paul reminds us to "Do everything without complaining and arguing…" (Philippians 2:14). "Everything" in the original language means *everything*, such as cleaning the toilets, staying up with your sick kid at night, navigating a tough work conversation, waiting in line at the bank. When we do it without complaining, we're more open to see the good in the season we're in and to embrace it.

It is important to note that venting and complaining are not necessarily the same. Getting things off our chest, letting our emotions out, and being honest with people can all be very healthy. With venting, there is a healthy consequence of letting off some steam and letting go of some things weighing on us. With complaining, it doesn't really result in letting go but in capturing even more pressure, which builds into a negative cycle.

A big part of complaining also comes back to developing healthy habits. The discipline to hold my tongue, to stop typing the whining e-mail, to reframe my attitude toward others is not easy, but it is something I can do so I don't miss out on the blessings of God right in front of me.

Solomon writes, "Yet God has made everything beautiful for its own time. He has planted eternity in the human heart, but even so, people cannot see the whole scope of God's work from beginning to end" (Ecclesiastes 3:11). The original Hebrew word here for "beautiful" can also be translated "appropriate" or "fair." Knowing God ordered the seasons of the earth can help us to trust Him; He is able to also appropriately and fairly order the seasons of our individual lives and the seasons of human life as a whole, even when we don't always understand what He is up to.

TIME OF OUR LIVES

Experiencing the beauty in our present season means we need to seriously consider what season we are in and why. The way the Greeks looked at time can help equip us in this. They had two different words for time. One was *chronos*, from which we get "chronology." This is the time of the clock, the calendar, and the smart phone. This is what we usually think of when it comes to time. And chronos time is always slipping away. We go from one task to another, always consuming time. This is where many of us live, moving from one thing to the next, always checking to see what time it is.

The other word they had was *kairos*, which is more about time as an opportunity and a gift. The question here we must ask ourselves becomes, "What is the purpose of this time I've been given? What's the purpose for this current season of my life?"

Maybe you're in college and working and interning and launching out into the world. You're incredibly busy with stuff and activities. It's okay. It's a season. This is the season where you learn and you get the most out of your educational experiences. There will be other seasons where you can do other things.

Or you might be taking on new jobs, and there may be

seasons where you have to make sacrifices for your family. Some are starting new companies and going through seasons of sacrifice to get it off the ground. Others may be in a place of retirement. There are different priorities and opportunities both for yourself and for your kids and grandkids.

What season are you in and what's the purpose for it? The hard thing is to make sure to manage the seasons. Solomon saw people rushing from season to season, trying to avoid the bad times, taking the good times for granted by always looking for what's next. He says, "Enjoy prosperity while you can, but when hard times strike, realize that both come from God" (Ecclesiastes 8:14). He reminds us that when the storms come, and they will come, we must find shelter in God.

LIVE IN SEASON

Sometimes a hard season feels like it will never end. A few years ago I went through a season where I watched my parents' health fade and saw them both pass within a couple years. We were right in the middle of the recession and the housing collapse in America, and the leadership challenges at church just felt completely overwhelming. On top of this, I felt attacked by a group of people who didn't understand the whole situation we were navigating, and I wasn't at liberty to tell them. It was a tough season.

Looking back, God taught me to cherish the days we have with loved ones. He helped me redefine my view of success because life is short and ultimately loving God and people are what matter most. He taught me to trust in Him as my defender rather than defending myself, to wait patiently for the full story to emerge and to rest in Him. He was building character in me that I draw on today.

This is what James was talking about when he said, "Dear brothers and sisters, when troubles come your way, consider it an opportunity for great joy. For you know that when your faith is tested, your endurance has a chance to grow" (James 1:2–3).

When you are in a season that's challenging and you're suffering, recognize it and seek shelter in it, but don't miss God's greater purpose. God uses the challenging seasons of our lives to grow us. James goes on to say when your endurance is fully developed, you will be perfect and complete, needing nothing. When we rush from season to season, we don't give God time to work. When stuff is hard, that's when He's most active, not least. Ironically, often when we feel Him the least, He is doing the most.

When you're frustrated at work and things that used to be so easy are now so hard, He's perfecting you. When you're struggling in a relationship with a child, spouse, or friend and everything seems to be falling apart, God is completing you. When you feel like you lost that thing that is most dear, most important to you, God is there working, giving you all you really need. And if you stick with it, if you live in season rather that rushing to what's next, in the future you will look back and say: That was the season I grew and learned. That was the season I found God was with me even in the darkest times.

In his book *Spiritual Rhythm: Being with Jesus Every Season of Your Soul,* Mark Buchanan encourages us to search out two things no matter what season we are in: Christ's presence and Christ's wisdom. He writes, "If we are to bear much fruit—if that's the goal of the Christian life—then the best model for spiritual maturity is seasons. Fruit grows in seasons, and all seasons are necessary for growing it. And seasons are as much about what is not happening as what is. It has as much to do with inactivity as with activity, waiting as with working, barrenness as with abundance, dormancy as with vitality. For everything there is a season."[15]

Whatever season you are in right now, look for where Jesus is showing up and how you might make the most of each season. What is He teaching you? What is He revealing? How can you grow and celebrate the good things in this season? What does it look like to wait patiently in this season?

IN HIS TIME

When the leaves turn, we know the season is changing, but sometimes we can't see things clearly in our lives. We forget God is always working in every season. I recently received a letter that reminded me of how He makes things beautiful in His time.

When I first came to faith, I had a lot of friends that I did crazy things with. I was really frustrated in that season because no matter how much I tried, I was not able to help even one of them see the need to turn to God. They stayed firmly planted in the drug culture, even as God led me to college to study to become a pastor. I prayed for them all the time. I tried to share my faith with them, but for the most part nothing happened. I was planting, but I was not seeing any harvest.

Over twenty years later, I received a letter from a county jail in Texas. One of my old high school party friends whom I had shared my faith with many times wrote to tell me he found my book *Uncensored Grace* in the prison library. In the book I describe my bedroom where I first surrendered to God. My friend knew that room well from the many times we'd partied together. He writes, "I remember that back room quite well. I remember the day you told me you had laid it all down. I should have taken your lead then....I am completely surrendered to Christ for the first time in my life. Your book is a real encouragement....I'm so thankful you laid it all down and I'm starting to understand what it means to be crucified with Christ. As unlikely as it may seem, your words made quite an impact, merely by the way you've lived your life..."

I read that letter and felt such wonder toward God. You just don't know how God will use the current season you're in. Twenty years from now, you may hear from a friend who remembers something you did, said, or wrote that made a difference in his or her life. You can't always see it now, you don't know what God is up to, but He is working and He is faithful. Sometimes He'll surprise you with a reminder like my letter that He never stops working, even when we move on with life. Without realizing it, God took what was planted and eventually moved it into a season of harvest.

Solomon concludes with a refrain that reminds us to take life in stride: "So I concluded there is nothing better than to be happy and enjoy ourselves as long as we can. And people should eat and drink and enjoy the fruits of their labor, for these are gifts from God" (Ecclesiastes 3:12–13).

Don't rush from the bad seasons to the good seasons or from the good seasons to the next season, hoping it's better.

Slow down.

Live in the moment.

Be where you are—*right now*.

Every season has its place, no matter how much we rush. Every season has a purpose, whether we realize it or not. God makes everything beautiful in its time, even the seasons that seem to envelop us in darkness. We can rest in the shelter of His loving arms and know that this, too, shall pass. As Max Lucado noted, if you're in a relationship with God, "everything will work out in the end. If it's not working out, it's not the end!"[16]

Chapter Five
Yes to Impact

No man can sincerely try to help another without helping himself.

—*Ralph Waldo Emerson*

"It's *not* fair!"

My kids are always saying this when they think their sibling got a better deal, or when their game gets taken away, or when the channel gets switched, or really when anything happens that doesn't go their way. We feel this way at work when our boss takes the credit for the project we spent sixty-hour weeks putting together or when a less-qualified candidate gets the promotion we were pursuing. We feel it at home when we think we're carrying more of the family responsibilities or when we watch our neighbor (who works from home a few hours a week) pull up in a brand-new luxury sports car.

Then we look around at our world and we see all the craziness and injustice, with criminals getting richer and honest people suffering for telling the truth. We watch people get trampled over by the greedy and powerful; those who are down often get kicked even lower. And it all seems so unfair.

UNFAIREST OF THEM ALL

When Solomon looked out at all the craziness and injustice in the world, this sentiment just grew to the point of exasperation. He writes, "Again, I observed all the oppression that takes place under the sun. I saw the tears of the oppressed, with no one to comfort them. The oppressors have great power, and their victims are helpless. So I concluded that the dead are better off than the living. But most fortunate of all are those who are not yet born. For they have not seen all the evil that is done under the sun" (Ecclesiastes 4:1–3).

Solomon looked to the courts and politicians and saw they were all crooked. People longed for justice but couldn't find any. He looked across the land and saw evil people getting away with murder while good people went hungry. He saw incompetent people getting huge promotions while the people who actually knew what they were doing got no recognition. He looked at life and saw some people have it really, really good, but most people didn't. Sound familiar?

In these verses and many others in Ecclesiastes, it's like he's throwing his arms in the air and screaming, "Life. Isn't. Fair!"

Throughout the Bible there's a recurring theme of oppression; specifically, oppression against those who can't defend themselves. It comes in many forms: bondage, slavery, human rights taken away, property confiscated, life threatened, discouragement, and fear. It involves cheating one's neighbor of something, defrauding him, or robbing him, or making an unjust gain. Bible scholar Iain Provan said oppression is, "the abuse of power, financial and otherwise, perpetrated on those who are not so powerful and are indeed vulnerable— the poor, widows, orphans, and strangers."[17]

But we don't need Solomon or the Bible to tell us about oppression and life's unfairness, do we? We can just scan the headlines, turn on the TV, or scan our Facebook feed. Bad stuff is happening. The world is full of people who need help. That's not the question.

The question is what do we do about it? Can we do *anything*? Isn't this problem above our pay grade? Don't we have enough problems of our own without trying to play super-hero and meet the needs of countless others? We can't help everyone, but how do we decide whom to help, how much to help, when to help, when not to help? And will anything we do really matter, or are we just wasting our time and resources fighting a losing battle against the truth that life isn't fair?

Have you ever had those thoughts? Ever struggled with wanting to help, but not knowing how? I've found that much of my attitude hinges on saying yes to God. When I drift from Him, I lose the bigger picture. I see the bad, but don't always see the good that God is bringing forth behind the scenes. I see the pain and want to throw my hands in the air in frustration, just like Solomon, rather than surrendering to God and partnering with Him in helping others.

However, when I open my heart to Him and seek to get out of the way for God to use me, I find a great joy in help-ing people. I don't have all the answers, but I do have one answer that has helped me as I face this issue in my own life: I can't help everyone, but I can help every "one" that God leads me to help. I don't have to take responsibility for saving the world—God's got that one under control despite appearances to the contrary. My calling is to help the neighbor, the coworker, the child, the homeless person, the senior in a nursing home, the single mom, the out-of-work dad who comes across my path on any given day.

And it's not just for the good of others or because God tells us to that we should help other people. Studies have shown that helping others is good for us and triggers the pleasure area of the brain. Neuroscientists James Rilling and Gregory Berns of Emory University recorded people's brain activity as they helped people out. They found that this activity triggered the portions of the brain associated with pleasure and receiving rewards. Dacher Kelter summarized their findings: "[H]elping others brings the same pleasure we get from the gratification of personal desire."[18] There is a physiological and spiritual joy in serving others. When we help someone else, life will still be unfair, but one life will be different. And that one life can affect countless others, and it will certainly affect our own.

CHECKING OUT

How do you react when you pull up to a stoplight and see a disheveled person standing there with a cardboard sign that says: HOMELESS. PLEASE HELP. GOD BLESS.? If you're like me, you may feel a little uncomfortable, not quite sure what to do. Do we give them a dollar? Do we wave them over and hand them an invite to church? Do we offer to buy them food? Do we avoid eye contact altogether as they slowly walk by, one foot away from the window? Do we do the radio check in the car? (You know what I'm talking about!)

Since we often don't know what to do, and since unfortunately we see them frequently in most urban areas, we may get desensitized and check out. Some homeless guys are responding to this by getting a bit more creative. One homeless man stood on the corner with this on his piece of cardboard: BOOGIEMAN ATE MY FAMILY. SPARE ANY CHANGE FOR NEW CLOSET DOOR? Another wrote: SPENT ALL MY MONEY ON CARDBOARD AND MARKER. And the most interesting: DESPERATE NEED OF HAIR WEAVE, PLEASE HELP.

These individuals know all too well that when we see a need long enough, we are tempted to just zone out. Stare straight ahead. Refuse to make eye contact. Check the radio or our phone until the problem passes by.

It's not that we don't care; we just don't always know *how* to care. There are too many people with so many needs that we can never help them all. We start to engage in a certain logic that goes something like this: If I give this guy a buck, then to be fair I'd need to give every homeless guy a buck, and I don't have that many bucks. If I volunteer one hour per week, they'll ask for two and I know they need four; that's more than I can give so I think I'll just keep my name and my time to myself. If I listen to this problem, I will have to listen to all their problems, and they have a *lot* of problems. I don't have the margin or the answers. I can't make life fair, so what's the point? Besides, doesn't the Bible say God helps those who help themselves?

This is a common response, but it isn't biblical. Nowhere in the Bible does it say God helps those who help themselves (that's actually Ben Franklin). But in countless places it talks about God's passion for the hurting, the poor, and the helpless. In Scripture we are called to mirror God's justice, for God loves the just (Psalm 37:28, Proverbs 28:5). So many of Jesus' works and miracles were for the poor, the sick, the needy. His work, along with being uniquely spiritual, was also very, very physical.

One of the most striking passages about our opportunity in helping others was spoken by Jesus as He describes a scene at the end of time. All the people of the earth stand before Him to give an account of their life, one group on His right and the other on His left. Here is what He says: "Then the King will say to those on his right, 'Come, you who are blessed by my Father, inherit the Kingdom prepared for you from the creation of the world. For I was hungry, and you fed me. I was thirsty, and you gave me a drink. I was a stranger, and you invited me into your home. I was naked, and you gave me clothing. I was sick, and you cared for me. I was in prison, and you visited me'" (Matthew 25:34–36).

The righteous are shocked. They have no idea how they served and visited Jesus in prison. They were just going about their lives, helping people one at a time. Then Jesus continues, "I tell you the truth, when you did it to one of the least of these my brothers and sisters, you were doing it to me!" (Matthew 25:40).

Helping others is a big deal with God, because when we show compassion to another person, we aren't just helping them, we are serving the God who saved us. We're showing thanks and gratitude to the One who helped us when we couldn't help ourselves. We are giving a little bit of what we have to the Savior who gave us His all. So even though the needs of others may wear us out, break our heart, make us suspicious, or make us feel inadequate, we can't ignore them. We can't just check out. It's too important to God and too vital to our faith. And what matters before what they do with your gift is your heart in giving it.

WINNING THE BATTLE

I recently had a mind-bending phone call with Dr. Scott Todd, who leads a movement called 58:, which is coordinating the efforts of poverty-fighting organizations into the world's largest unified effort to end extreme poverty. He's convinced that we can end extreme poverty in this generation. He shared a couple things that really rattled me.

The first is that we often default to Jesus' words: "You will always have the poor among you..." (John 12:8). Christians love to quote this verse, almost as a cop-out. For two thousand years it has tended to lower our expectations about the difference we can make. Scott asked me, "Have you ever really thought about who Jesus was speaking to when He said this?"

I said, "Uh, no." Honestly, those words sort of floated in isolation in my mind. Then Dr. Todd reminded me that Jesus said these words to Judas. It was just after Mary anointed Jesus with a jar of perfume worth about $45,000 in our economy, a year's wages, then or now. Judas was upset at Mary and notes that the perfume shouldn't have been wasted, but sold and the money given to the poor. Yet the Bible tells us that Judas' heart was really not for the poor. He was in charge of the disciples' money and often stole some for himself (John 12:6). So Jesus turns to Judas and essentially calls him out. He says, "Leave her alone. She did this in preparation for my burial. You will always have the poor among you, but you will not always have me" (John 12:7–8). I bet you could have heard a pin drop.

Todd built a compelling case. He contends that Jesus' statement is directed specifically to Judas; it was never intended as a blanket principle. He argues from the second half of Jesus' statement, "you will not always have me." If that statement was for us, then how do we reconcile it with the statement of Jesus' final commission: "I am with you always, even to the end of the age" (Matthew 28:20)?

Todd argues that both statements were specific to Judas. Jesus was teaching him a lesson and Judas would not always have Jesus with him. In fact, just after this scene we read that Judas goes over the edge and sells Jesus out. If the second part of Jesus' statement was specific to Judas, then the first part should be seen for what it is in the context of the moment and the conversation. At the very least, Todd challenged me to rethink my assumptions about poverty and the difference we can make.

The second thing he shared that surprised me was how much progress has been made in the last fifty years toward ending extreme global poverty. Owing to human greed and selfishness and the consequences of sin, there will always be poverty, but Todd believes we can end extreme poverty in this generation. He defines extreme poverty as life on less than $1.25 a day, where the basic needs of life are not met. He said: "In 1981, fifty-two percent of the world's population lived in extreme poverty. As of 2005, that number is twenty-six percent. We have cut the percentage of people living in extreme poverty in half! And we did it in one generation!"[19]

Todd is leading the charge to pool our resources toward closing the gap on the final 26 percent in this generation. He notes that even atheist researchers are admitting it is possible! If that's the case, then how much more should we as Christians pray and work toward this end since we see every person as made in God's image.

When I hung up the phone, I felt incredibly convicted and encouraged. I had not only lowered my expectations too much regarding the difference that could be made, but I also never realized how much progress we were making together. I thought of the kids that we sponsor in extreme poverty through Compassion International in a new light. We love our sponsored kids, and I've even had the chance to meet one of them, Melissa, and spend time with her in Ecuador. But I never realized the overall effect of actions like this reproduced millions of times by ordinary people.

Saying yes to God allows you to find satisfaction in helping others and resist the temptation to check out. It's a path that leads to guilt for today and regret for tomorrow. Don't refuse to help one person, because you can't help everyone. And realize if we all do our part, there can be a massive impact.

BURNING OUT AND BLOWING UP

Do you know any fixers? When stuff gets broken, they're the guy or gal you call and they can fix anything. When I was a kid, I used to think of myself as a fixer. The miracle material was scotch tape. If I got a hole in my socks, I'd just use scotch tape. If one of my toys broke, no problem, just get some tape. My mom complained that when I was growing up, she'd buy out the store of scotch tape just so I could fix everything. But when I grew up, I discovered something far superior to this childish solution for fixing broken things—duct tape!

Sometimes fixers, myself included, think they can fix people just as easily as a broken toy or a leaky pipe. We try to duct tape people. We hear about another person's struggles, we see a problem in the world, and we think to ourselves, *I'm gonna fix this.* I am going to once and for all get my struggling relative out of debt and get them on a budget. I am going to fix my boyfriend or husband and cure his addictions; my caring love will patch them right up. Those rebellious kids just need a good role model; if I'm just strong and consistent, always there when they need me, I can make it right.

The problem with duct tape thinking is you start to see yourself as the solution to everything. You take on more problems, more stress, more burdens until one day the load gets so huge, the demands so overwhelming, that you flame out. You quit. Nothing is working. None of the fixes are sticking. You feel like a complete failure when all you were trying to do was save a few people who had no one else to turn to.

I learned this firsthand after spending several years deeply involved with the homeless ministry. We would serve them food and encourage them in whatever way we could. I quickly came to realize that the homeless may be the most evangelized people in America. Every homeless person I met had Bible tracts in their pockets that somebody gave them, and they could often quote Scripture better than our volunteers. I kept trying to duct tape them together in my own power—more food, more resources, more Bible verses—and it never worked.

One day we were serving in a food line and a couple hundred homeless were all lined up under a nearby bridge. I was standing next to my friend Charlene, an awesome volunteer. She gave up time she didn't have to buy the food from the grocery store, prepare it, and coordinate the volunteers. On top of all this she was a mom, parent, employee, and college student. One of the homeless guys received the food on his plate she had lovingly prepared and huffed: "This looks awful. Is this all there is?"

Before I knew what happened, I just snapped. My fatigue and anger all boiled over at this man's attitude toward someone who had given so much. I jumped over the folding table, knocked his plate out of his hands a good ten feet, and pushed him. In a flash my fists were up and I was about to sock the guy in the jaw when he stumbled back and looked at me defeated. The weariness in his eyes just said it all. Here was a guy who had already had the life beaten out of him. He had nothing left to fight for. He stood under a bridge getting food from Christian people, and one of them, me, was about to knock him down again for complaining. Not exactly what Jesus would do.

Thankfully, by God's grace, I got hold of myself and didn't hit the guy. It was all horribly embarrassing, and I felt very ashamed. I apologized and walked away, feeling like an absolute loser. Over the coming weeks I realized that for the first time I was burning out. I had compassion fatigue. By trying in my own power to fix things, ultimately I had lost my focus on God. After that incident I took a long break from the homeless ministry and did some much-needed soul-searching.

Sometimes we get so committed to helping, so committed to saving, we forget that God is the one who truly heals and saves. As Jeremiah said, "O LORD, if you heal me, I will be truly healed; if you save me, I will be truly saved. My praises are for you alone!" (Jeremiah 17:14). You and I were never meant to save people. We do the helping and God does the healing. We do the serving and God does the saving. When we try to fix people, it really is like wrapping something with duct tape. It kinda works for a little while, but it ain't pretty and it never lasts. Duct tape is only designed to be a temporary solution at best. God is the one that saves. We are called to love and to help in the best way we know how.

EVERY SINGLE ONE

The way God calls us to help others is based on one person at a time. Among the millions and billions of people on this earth who need food, water, medicine, money, jobs, counseling, comfort, and the human touch, God doesn't expect you to meet all their needs. He only asks that you treat each one you encounter as He would treat them, as He has treated you.

I love a scene described in the Bible that happened in the early days of the church. Two leaders, Peter and John, are walking into the big public worship area of the Temple. This place is always busy with lots of foot traffic, and they're on the way to a prayer service when a man who's been crippled from birth is carried in and set down by one of the entrances so he can beg for money.

Basically, it's the biblical equivalent of our encountering a homeless guy carrying a cardboard sign. Do I throw the guy a buck? Or do I walk by, avoid eye contact, and tell myself he'll probably just spend it on alcohol anyway?

The text says that when the beggar saw "Peter and John about to enter, he asked them for some money. Peter and John looked at him intently, and Peter said, 'Look at us!' The lame man looked at them eagerly, expecting some money. But Peter said, 'I don't have any silver or gold for you. But I'll give you what I have. In the name of Jesus Christ the Nazarene, get up and walk!' Then Peter took the lame man by the right hand and helped him up. And as he did, the man's feet and ankles were instantly healed and strengthened. He jumped up, stood on his feet, and began to walk! Then, walking, leaping, and praising God, he went into the Temple with them" (Acts 3:3–8).

Here we see that, right off the bat, God put *one guy* in front of Peter and John to help. This was a busy place with lots of beggars and lots of needs, but this is the one that God put in their path and moved their hearts to help. They didn't ignore the person that God literally put at their feet.

This required them to stop and recognize the situation. Like most people then and now, they were busy and helping someone wasn't on the schedule. They had to make time and be willing to stop and engage.

They gave this man what they had. He holds out his hand and Peter tells him straight up, "I don't have money for you. There's not a thing I have to give, but what I have, I give you."

God isn't asking us to give what we don't have, but what we *do*. We don't always have money to give with bills to pay and mouths at home to feed. By the time you pay for your home, gas, and groceries and give to your church and other ministries, there may not be any left. We can't give what we don't have, but that doesn't mean we can't do anything. We might be able to give a friend a ride or lend an ear to listen and empathize. And the last time I checked, prayer still doesn't cost anything.

It doesn't have to be a burden if we're willing to give honestly and simply what we've been given. Some of us are strapped for time. If we have a job, family, especially young kids, and a home to take care of, we may not have hardly any time to give, but we may have an extra spot at our table. Maybe we have an old car in the driveway that we don't use that's dripping oil and staining the concrete, but could do a world of good for someone else. Maybe we have influence and can simply make a call and put in a good word for someone else looking for work or help.

Peter says he'll give the man what he has and "In the name of Jesus Christ the Nazarene, get up and walk!" (Acts 3:6). And the man is healed. But notice that even though Peter was the one helping, it was the power of Jesus that did the healing. Even a guy who had walked with Jesus himself, a founding father of Christianity who performed many miracles in his lifetime, realized that it was not his efforts that healed and saved, it was the work of God. Peter let this guy know it was all about Jesus.

What is the first thing this guy does with his brand-new legs? He walks into the temple to go worship with Peter and

John. This guy goes to church! He praises God. And that's the ultimate goal of helping someone, whether it's a family member you see every day, some random person God brings into your life, or people in a country you will never see or visit. We point them to Jesus so that more people will see, know, and praise God. It's not to ease our guilt, to make us feel good, or even to make the world a perfect place. The way we find satisfaction in helping others is to point them to God so He can heal and save them.

If you have money and God calls you to give money to someone, give it. Don't loan it and keep tabs, just release it. Anything else will rob your joy. If God calls you to give time, give it, but set some limits. If you're a parent or a spouse, your family needs your time, too. If you have a job or a business, you need time for that, too. You need time to sleep and rest. *Give the gifts you have, not the gifts you don't have.*

When you see a homeless person on the street and feel compelled to help, then do something. My friends who used to be homeless tell me never to give money to a guy on the street. It often perpetuates suffering for them if they use it for drugs or alcohol. So if you have time, buy them some food. If you don't, give them meal cards. One friend of mine who came off the streets rides in his car with McDonald's gift certificates so he's always ready to help.

If you are trying to help someone with an addiction or a challenging behavioral issue, seek help. Many churches offer recovery programs. Bribe them with food and see if they will come along. Get around people that know how to help people deal with their issues.

There are some amazing churches and organizations out

there that do great work. We love sponsoring people through Compassion International, both individually and as a church. But it's not an out. I don't think that because I give to the church and I support charities, I don't need to help when God brings that one person into my life. If we just give money and nothing else, we'll be missing out on something great God wants to do in our lives.

HELPING THE HOPELESS

It's important to realize that we're not called to help only those people who agree with us or even want to be helped. Patrick Green was a taxi driver in Austin, Texas. He was also an outspoken atheist constantly challenging any religious displays on government property. He had recently filed a lawsuit to remove the nativity scene from the courthouse area when a doctor told him that he needed eye surgery to remove some cataracts and repair a detached lens. Patrick couldn't afford the surgery and shortly after his diagnosis, he lost his job due to failing vision and was left with the challenge of supporting himself and his wife of thirty-three years.

That's when Jessica Crye, a Christian woman who read about Greene's troubles in the paper, went to members of her church and asked if they would be willing to donate money to help Greene. They ended up raising $400 in donations for Greene, which left him "flabbergasted" that a group of Christians would do this for an atheist.[20]

The whole experience caused him to question his long-held beliefs and wrestle with God. In the days since the story broke, he's confessed his faith in Christ, then renounced it.

Then declared he wants to be a Baptist minister, and then backed away. He's a complicated guy, and according to his new pastor and mentor, there's still a lot he needs to figure out, but there's no denying the fact that a simple act of kindness did what no amount of arguing could ever accomplish. It brought him face to face with the God who heals and the God who saves.

Green has not only rescinded his lawsuit to remove the nativity from the courthouse, but agreed to buy a star for the tree if someone can just show him where to plug it in. He also plans to write a book called *The Real Christians of Henderson County*.

Someday you and I will be standing before Jesus and he'll call out, "I was hungry, and you fed me. I was thirsty, and you gave me a drink.... I was sick, and you cared for me."

And we will respond, "When did we ever see you hungry and feed you? Or thirsty and give you something to drink?"

Jesus responds, "When you did it to one of the least of these my brothers and sisters you were doing it to me!" (Matthew 25:35–37, 40).

Life will never be fair until heaven. But until then, we can advance His presence one act at a time, one person at a time. When we say yes to God, we refuse to accept the unfairness of life and remind ourselves—and others—of a greater divine reality.

Chapter Six

Yes to Friendship

Friendship is unnecessary, like philosophy, like
art.... It has no survival value; rather it is one of
those things which give value to survival.

—*C. S. Lewis*

"Can you spot me on the bench press?"

The biggest guy I'd ever seen in a gym was looking directly at me. I turned around to double-check and make sure no one else was behind me, but it was just the two of us in the basement weight room of an old school YMCA. No trendy music was playing in the background, no rows of treadmills hooked to TVs; this was a no-frills gym and the only sound was the low buzz of fluorescent lightbulbs. The guy was about 5-foot-10 with midlength choppy black hair, brown eyes, and somewhere north of 250 pounds. Seriously, he looked like a shorter version of the Hulk.

"How 'bout a spot?" he repeated as if talking to someone who didn't speak English. I agreed because what else do you say to a guy this big? I had never seen so much weight on a bench press bar. When you are "spotting" someone, you stand behind them while they bench press and help them guide the bar up in case they get in trouble and cannot finish a rep. I was already nervous about whether I could handle the kind of weights this dude must lift when I watched him stack more and more plates on the ends of the bar.

Nonetheless, I walked over behind the bench press as the Hulk took his place on the bench and lifted the massive bar off the rests. It sagged just a little in the middle, which was unnerving. He did two impressive reps, making an even more impressive grunt each time. Little guys with small weights who grunt at the gym are annoying, but guys who look like this can do whatever they want and look, well, cool.

On his third rep he made it halfway up and just stopped in midair. He grunted again, more primal, then the bar dropped an inch and he blurted out, "Need a little help here." I reached down and tugged on the bar with all my strength.

Nothing. The bar wouldn't budge at all. In fact, it dropped a little. His face was red, his eyes were bulging, his teeth were clenched, and he repeated desperately, "Help here." I tugged again with everything in my power and joined him in the grunting for effect, but the bar dropped *down* another inch, almost touching his chest. All I could say was, "I've got nothing else."

He looked at me like he was going to kill me and then did a professional weightlifter move that I'll never forget. With lightning speed he slid his back to the left, somehow held his left arm in position, and dropped his right arm so that the bar hit the right side of the bench at enough of an angle that all the weight slid off the right side of the bar.

With the weight gone on the right side, the bar then flew to the left with tremendous split-second force. He rotated his back to the right, dropping his left hand so that the bar would hit the bench on the left side, causing the weights to slide off again. He stood up and threw the empty bench press bar across the gym and turned around and looked at me. It all happened in a blink. I stood there in amazement and thought, *I'm going to die in the basement weight room of an old YMCA.*

I managed a weak apology and he paced around, breathing loudly and clinching and loosening his fists. Then he came over and said, "We're going to start working out together."

Uh, okay...

This began my first training regimen with a partner. We met every day at the gym around noon and we became friends. His name was John and he loved to push me, especially when he found out I was a Christian. He'd say, "If you were a real Christian, you'd give me four more curls!" or "Three more chin-ups if you really love Jesus!" Somehow I always felt like getting those reps in was a way of showing him the reality of my faith, so I'd give it all I had...and pray!

I remember many days when I would walk out to my car, and my arms were so shot from lifting weights that it took both hands to get the car key in the door. At night I'd have to ask Lori to help me lift my hand to brush my teeth! How pathetic!

Over time I became stronger than ever before because of my friendship with John. I developed muscles in places they'd never been, and soon I was in the best shape of my entire life. My unlikely friend transformed my physical condition.

TRANSFORMERS

That's the power of someone in our lives encouraging us, challenging us, and pushing us to grow and develop. He saw things in me that I couldn't always see and he believed I could do more than I ever thought. This is what friends do. And when my friend John moved away, it wasn't the same. I'd still hit the gym, but less often, and my workouts were halfhearted. My muscles began a long atrophy.

The life of faith is like this. When we begin to live in God's yes, we don't do it in isolation. Saying yes to God means saying yes to others. Together we can grow and develop to become all that God desires. We push each other to keep learning, keep praying, keep living toward God.

In his memoir, Solomon has the wisdom to look back and see the importance of other people for so many things in life. He writes, "Two people are better off than one, for they can help each other succeed" (Ecclesiastes 4:9). With the synergy of teamwork and relationships, two people can accomplish more than twice as much as one. There is a momentum that happens when we work together and we help each other succeed. Despite all of his weariness and fatigue, Solomon saw clearly that so much of life hinges on friendships.

NORMAL AND POSSIBLE

My mom used to drive me crazy when she'd say that who I hung around was who I would become. I argued with her like all teenagers argue with their parents, but looking back, she couldn't have been more right. I'm convinced one of the best predictors of your future is your friends.

I ran around with some wild friends in high school. Many of them ended up in jail or prison. Saying yes to God made the difference in my life, but not in complete isolation. When I said yes to God, I began to interact with other people who also said yes to God. They had different values, and just by being around them, I learned how to live sober, how to face conflict without running to drugs or alcohol, how to treat other people with respect and kindness, and how to depend on God.

The influence of our friends affects every aspect of our lives, even in ways we don't perceive. Harvard sociologist Nicholas Christakis found through research that even obesity is a partially shared activity. He found that if you have obese friends, you will be 57 percent more likely to be obese yourself.[21]

The influence is subtle, but real. Our friends determine how we define what is normal, from diet to exercise to family dynamics. Pretty soon we view the behavior we're around as the standard even if it's unhealthy or blatantly destructive and leads to all kinds of problems. So simply having a friend is not necessarily good for us; it all depends on the kind of friends we have. It isn't that *any* two are better than one; the *right* two are better than one. As the writer of Proverbs concludes: "Walk with the wise and become wise; associate with fools and get in trouble" (13:20).

My friend Joseph Grenny and his colleagues have done groundbreaking research on how we change from a sociological perspective. In their book *Change Anything: The New Science of Personal Success,* they point to the influences that shape our lives. Changing habits isn't a mysterious secret anymore; they have scientifically studied and determined what it takes to change behavior. And one of the most important aspects of life change is the friends in our lives.

The authors call negative relationships accomplices. These are people we may really enjoy hanging out with, but they have a bad influence on us. Their negative perspective toward work taints our perspective toward work; their lack of discipline causes us to slack in discipline. Their tendency to smoke or drink or whatever reinforces our tendency to do the same things. Our friends don't always influence us intentionally, but they are accomplices nonetheless.

Those that influence us positively, to stay on the path and confront destructive habits, are classified as true friends. When it comes to these friends, we need both coaches and fans. Coaches are those people who give us insight and perspective. They share wisdom, experience, encouragement, and support. They help us face our own weaknesses. Coaches can be formal or informal, individuals we meet for lunch or leaders we hear at seminars or authors who inspire us with their words. Their influence comes into our lives in many ways—through books, tapes, seminars, classes, and conversations.

As Joseph and his colleagues put it: "If you're finding it particularly tough to change, it's very possible you have people around you who actively hold you accountable to a bad habit."[22] If you find yourself around coworkers who hate their job and constantly complain and whine about work, you'll likely find yourself depressed about work as well. It's tough to overcome the accomplices in your life.

For example, when surrounded by negative coworkers, imagine what could happen if you began to seek out informal coaches who seem positive, who seem to love their work. What if you invited them to lunch or purposely got around them during break time? You are informally putting yourself around another set of influences that can begin to shape your attitude. You also begin to distance yourself from all the negativity of those who don't like their job.

Spiritually, if you're drifting in your faith or down in your church, look around you. It may be that those around you have influenced you in a negative cycle. What would happen if you got into another small group with people who were growing and excited about the things of God? What if you got around people who shared your values and your faith? Those people would begin to shape you in more ways than you would consciously even frame up.

We need coaches and we need fans. Both may be personal friends, but fans go a step further. They cheerlead us and inspire us to keep going, to not give up, to dig deeper, to realize we can reach higher. Fans take the time to tell you the great things you are doing. When you hang up after a phone call with them, you suddenly feel like you can tackle the challenges in front of you head on.

So as much as I hate to admit it, Mom was right. We often become an average of the people that we spend the most time with. Have you found this to be true in your life? Who are the handful of people you spend the most time with? What kind of people are they? Do they mentor you through their life as a coach or a fan? Is this someone you would even want your kids to hang around if they were the same age?

Think about your influence in their lives. Are you encouraging them? Are you a coach or a fan, or maybe even an accomplice? Two of the right friends are better than one because we help each other rise up and succeed.

SMILE OF THE SECOND CHANCE

As much as it makes us uncomfortable sometimes, we all need other people. Solomon describes another benefit of having a friend this way: "If one person falls, the other can reach out and help. But someone who falls alone is in real trouble" (Ecclesiastes 4:10). Friends will be there for you when you fail, when you blow it, when everybody else has gone away. Nobody should have to struggle through the valleys of life alone.

One of the places where I've witnessed the life-lifting power of friendships is, surprisingly, in a prison. Granted, nobody wants to be in prison. It's a horrible place and often a dangerous environment. So to meet the many needs of the inmates, our church began to start small churches behind the bars of several prisons. These church campuses are launched in partnership with *God Behind Bars* and serve under prison chaplains. We provide volunteers as well as a recording of our weekend music and teaching to be shown on a large video screen. Small groups gather in Christ-focused twelve-step recovery groups.

When we began, we weren't sure anybody would participate, but from the beginning we were filling up all the seats the prison provided. For Christmas one year, we went into a women's prison for a live event. While I was familiar with prison ministry, nothing prepared me for the passion and joy in this second-chance community.

As hundreds of women walked into the service, my wife and I greeted them. We immediately saw the faces of people who had been rescued by Jesus from bitterness, loneliness, hate, and addiction. They carried well-used Bibles, many of which were gifts from our church. When the service started and these women rose to sing, their voices were louder than any rock concert I've ever attended. It was just beautiful, and I didn't mind that my ears rang for days.

Most of them had come to faith in Jesus through prison services our church held. We recognized one of the inmates from the news, someone charged in a high-profile murder. Others were there for every other kind of crime. But they came to faith, grew in their faith, and served each other together.

When I got up to speak, I looked out at some 400 women, all of them smiling back at me. Crazy as it sounds, what struck me in that moment is that virtually every woman in the service had missing teeth. These were young women—many in their twenties, thirties, and forties, and yet many were visibly missing one or more front teeth.

I asked a key volunteer why, and he said that in the prison if there was a cavity or dental issue, it was often cheaper to just pull their teeth rather than fix them. At first it angered me that we'd take a twenty-five-year-old woman who had messed up and pull her teeth and expect her to just bounce back when she gets out of the system.

But then I looked out at hundreds of ladies smiling ear to ear, their eyes closed, singing to Jesus with gratitude. They didn't care. If you didn't have teeth, you'd be tempted to close your mouth, especially to a group of people from the outside, but they smiled unselfconsciously the entire time. I call it the smile of the second chance—nothing to prove, nothing to lose, just a forgiven person who has received a new beginning in Jesus. It was an unbelievable service.

We were there to help them up, but what I saw in this community was their willingness to say yes to God and experience His help, which in turn allowed them to help each other up. I met many volunteers who drove a long way out to the prison each week to pour into these women. These amazing volunteers also meet many of them at the gate when they are released, give them a *Fresh Start* kit with basic supplies, and begin to help them with résumés, job skills, and places to live. They are true friends!

It reminded me that no matter how hurt or broken we become, no matter how low we fall, it is never too late to turn to God and the church community for help. The Hebrew word Solomon uses for "to fall" has a wide range of meaning. The image here is one of travelers on the road where people often fall into danger, damage, or destruction. All around us are people who fall into divorce, illness, addiction, family crises, or scandal.

True friends offer a hand rather than a foot; they reach out and take hold of hurting people and help them back on their feet. They ensure that we don't walk alone, don't face depression alone, don't go through the death of a loved one alone, or don't sit up at night worrying about a spouse serving on the military battlefield alone. When we fall and a friend helps us up, we, too, can smile the smile of the second chance.

COLD NIGHTS

Solomon continues to describe the power and benefits of friendship. He says, "Likewise, two people lying close together can keep each other warm. But how can one be warm alone?" (Ecclesiastes 4:11). The obvious point is that travelers together would be warm on cold nights if they slept close together. Spiritually, friends can help provide warmth in the winter seasons of our lives. They encourage us, listen to us, and share our dreams with us. These friends warm us because they're authentic in their care and concern.

One of the History Channel's most popular shows is *Pawn Stars,* filmed in a pawn shop in downtown Las Vegas. The premise is simple: people bring valuable items into the shop, and Rick, Big Hoss, and the Old Man offer cash money to buy them.

If you watch the show, you know there are a lot of factors that go into determining how much an item is worth, but the first thing the guys always want to know is this: *Is it real?* Is it an authentic Super Bowl ring or a knockoff? Is it a genuine Rolex or an imitation? A genuine Picasso sketch or an art student's best attempt? No matter how beautiful, awesome, or significant an item appears to be, the *Pawn Stars* won't let it in their shop if you can't prove its authenticity. They know that true value starts with what's real.

So they are always on the lookout for people trying to trick them, people pushing items that look good, but aren't. And the same can be true of our relationships. We think appearance is what matters most. Presentability. We want to look good. We want to hang around with the cool kids, the hip crowd. But true value and true friendship start with being authentic. If we want real relationships in our life, we have to be real with others, and usually that means not looking our best. At times, admitting our worst. Imitations may look good but ultimately they aren't worth squat.

To experience authentic friendship, we must engage in deeper levels of communication. At the first level of communication, there is simply information, where we share facts and observations. Everybody does this; it's basic, even with someone passing by on the street. We ask someone on the street the time; they tell us. We ask a friend what happened and they relay details, facts, and data about the event. We ask our parents and they tell us about the weather.

Obviously, we need to share information, but if you only share information, you're stuck on the bunny slopes of being real. You're splashing in the kiddie pool of communication. You need to lose the floaties and wade out farther. You need to move from information to opinions.

With opinions you're not just saying what you know, you're saying what you think about what you know. How you feel about what you know. We don't usually share opinions with strangers, but we do share them with acquaintances. People we've met. People we work with. We also share opinions with friends, but that is not what makes them a true friend, although refusing to, or not sharing an opinion, means the friendship is stalling out a bit.

What makes a friendship deeper is when we communicate about our true feelings, and not just our socially acceptable or "appropriate" ones. When we honestly describe our fears and anxieties, our selfish instincts, and our grandest dreams.

Think about the people you would be willing to admit your deepest hopes to. People you could trust with stuff that really scares or embarrasses you. If you have someone like that in your life, he or she is your true friend.

Everyone wants to have a friend like that. A community in which they can be real. But the truth is, most of us don't. Facebook floods us with information. Twitter bombards us with one-liners from our families and friends. Skype and texts keep us in constant communication. But few people have the courage to share, and keep sharing hopes, dreams, and fears.

If you want to have that kind of friendship, then pray God will show you that kind of friend, pray God will make you that kind of friend, and take a risk with someone you trust and share with them. In this community we find warmth and encouragement in the cold of life.

Helen Keller said, "Walking with a friend in the dark is better than walking alone in the light." We all want that kind of friend, one that walks with us through the darkness and the light. So we need to be that kind of friend with others—our kids, siblings, parents, spouses, and those special people God brings into our lives who walk with us no matter how dark things get.

Solomon says, "It is better to be a poor but wise youth than an old and foolish king who refuses all advice. Such a youth could rise from poverty and succeed. He might even become king, though he has been in prison. But then everyone rushes to the side of yet another youth who replaces him. Endless crowds stand around him, but then another generation grows up and rejects him, too. So it is all meaningless—like chasing the wind" (Ecclesiastes, 4:13–16).

It doesn't matter how far you go in life or how popular you get. You can go from a prison to a throne, but eventually the crowd wants someone else, the throne goes to another, and what are you left with? Popularity, success, fame, honor—they are all here today, gone tomorrow. Meaningless—like chasing after the wind. None of it is real.

What is the real thing? The people you came from. The people you go with. The people who stay to the end.

GOT YOUR BACK

True friends not only provide support and warmth, but they also offer shelter and protection. Sometimes this is in the form of a safe place to share what's on your heart or to just be understood. Sometimes this is literally someone who's got your back.

I was reminded of this when I was standing outside of our auditorium at church in a public area between services. A guy came up to me with a blue shirt, torn-off sleeves showing lots of tattoos, and slicked-back black hair. He was in good shape, about 6-foot-2 and he was raging mad. I had never met him but he just started yelling at me. His beef wasn't with our church, which he had never attended, but all churches. He said he hated what religion was about and hated me because I was a representative of Christianity. (Yes, I did find it odd that he chose to come to a church just to tell me this.)

He got louder and louder and I thought he was going to take my head off. At any moment I was prepared for the guy to swing at me. I concentrated on staying completely relaxed and did my best to talk him down for about ten minutes.

Eventually I experienced what the Bible says, "A gentle answer turns away wrath" (Proverbs 15:1, NIV). The guy settled down, said his piece, and left.

After he walked away, I began to shake. This was an intense moment. Then I turned around and I'll never forget what I saw. My friends, who I didn't even know were there, were all around me about fifteen to twenty feet back. Some were leaning, others were sitting very casually, nothing that would look threatening.

To my right there was a police officer in plain clothes. On the other side was a member of our city's SWAT team. In the corner was a former member of the special forces. On another side was a friend you wouldn't want to meet in an alley after dark under the wrong circumstances. These were my friends and they all came up to me afterward and nodded, saying, "We had your back." That's what friends do; they have your back. I was so thankful.

As Solomon says, "A person standing alone can be attacked and defeated, but two can stand back-to-back and conquer" (Ecclesiastes 4:12). The image is powerful. We all have blind spots. We are all vulnerable, but with a friend, we have someone to battle through life with us and someone who will fight for us.

A few years ago one man in our church was in a serious car accident and broke both his hands. They were casted from the tips of his fingers to his elbows. He wasn't able to type, get dressed on his own, drive, eat, bathe, or do any of the other daily activities that we sometimes take for granted. In addition to working full time and mothering their kids, his wife was in school to be a physician's assistant, and now she found herself driving her husband to physical therapy four times a week.

The first time he showed up to church after the accident, and saw a friend from his small group, things began to change. He wrote to me and said, "When this friend saw me with my new fashionable gloves, his mouth dropped. He immediately said, 'What can we do to help you?' Those words still ring in my heart. For me, it was always difficult to ask for help. I think sometimes it's much easier to give than to receive help from others because our pride gets in our way. Under my breath I muttered a few things that I would need help with."

People jumped in. They began to give him rides to and from work to help out his wife. They dropped off meals. They babysat their kids. Others prayed and offered encouragement.

He writes, "I cannot begin to express the gratitude and love that we feel for our church family. They all became an extension of the Lord's hands in my life when my own hands were worthless. . . . I now have full use of all my fingers and honestly think that the accident was the best thing that could have happened to me because it showed me how close we as Christians are supposed to be." He went through a horrible thing but he didn't go through it alone. There were people there to walk with him.

Solomon observes, "Three are even better, for a triple-braided cord is not easily broken" (Ecclesiastes 4:12). If you are standing alone in your life right now, you are incredibly vulnerable. In a spiritual sense, who is watching your back? Is there anyone who has the right to ask you: How are you doing with your relationship with God? How are you doing with your faith? Are you staying faithful in the church community? What are you wrestling with as far as temptations in your life?

They are the kind of friends who say, "We won't let you go off the road." If they see pride or arrogance in you, if they see things develop in you that are unhealthy, they are going to pull you aside and say, "We're your friends and we're watching your back. You need to deal with this area in your life and we'll help you."

The other question is, "Whose back are *you* watching?" It's a two-way street. We all need at least one person in our lives that we can really talk with and interact with about the deeper things in our lives.

RELATIONSHIP MODE

I want you to imagine you just got the most amazing news of your life. Think about the handful of people you would tell first. And now think honestly, how much time did I actually spend with them this week? As a dad and husband I struggle with this. It's so easy to let work and professional relationships dominate my schedule. Ultimately, I had to make some hard choices to be around work a little less so I could be around home a little more. It doesn't matter how important you say someone is to you; if they aren't on the calendar and in your life, you aren't living for the real thing.

It's an age-old problem that Solomon saw even in his time. "I observed yet another example of something meaningless under the sun. This is the case of a man who is all alone, without a child or a brother, yet who works hard to gain as much wealth as he can. But then he asks himself, 'Who am I working for? Why am I giving up so much pleasure now?' It is all so meaningless and depressing" (Ecclesiastes 4:7–8).

Here's a guy who looks up one day and realizes he has lots of stuff, but no community and—did you catch it—no pleasure. He asks a great question, "Who am I working for?" And we should all ask that question, too. We need to get real with our time. Where is all of it going? To relationships that can bring us joy, warmth, and protection, or is it all going toward something that ultimately will be meaningless?

One big challenge to friendships is what I call LCD ADD—technology-induced attention deficit disorder. The culprit is the smart phone. It makes us do crazy stuff like text our friends when we're out with our spouse, or text our spouse when we're out with our friends. It tempts you to check Facebook and Twitter when you're out with your *actual* friends in the three-dimensional world.

These are called smart phones, but if you let them steal the attention of the person you are spending time with, they become really dumb phones. Don't let your phone rob you of the Real Thing sitting in front of you. Your friend. Your brother. Your child. Your spouse. Don't succumb to LCD ADD. In our marriage Lori and I say that when the phone is off, it is now in relationship mode. Turn off the power to your phone, turn on the power of relationship. It's the only cure for LCD ADD.

If you're like me when you really want something, you find a way to make it happen. And the bigger it is, the more you plan. In fact, just picking up a pencil and a piece of paper and writing down a plan for your relationships may be the single most effective thing you can do in building those relationships. As four-time *New York Times* best-selling author Joseph Grenny and his colleagues concluded: "Repeated studies show that simply writing down a plan increases your chance of success by more than thirty percent."[23]

We often have plans such as a vacation plan, a new home plan, a retirement plan, or a job plan. We even have dinner plans, but when it comes to friendships, relationships, or community, we have no plan!

So take a moment to think one up. It can be really simple—for example, one Friday a month we have dinner with friends. Every other week I'm going to have lunch with my best friend. Every weeknight I'm going to read to my kids. At dinnertime we turn off the TV, turn off the phones, and talk.

For some of you, a good plan might be to try out a small group for the first time at church. Or to give a group you've been to another try. No matter what plan you think up, it's better than no plan. We need to get intentional about our relationships. Friendship is the real thing. It brings value to everything else in life and is one of the things we cherish most at the end of our lives.

Chapter Seven
Yes to Contentment

> Contentment is that inward, quiet, gracious frame
> of spirit, freely submitting to and taking pleasure
> in God's disposal in every condition.
> —*Jeremiah Burroughs*

Thanks to the invention of digital recording and playback, my kids made it many years without watching many non-fast-forwarded thirty-second commercials. I can still remember all of us sitting in our living room watching a favorite program on "live TV" when suddenly it cut to a commercial. Since it was a live broadcast and not recorded on our DVR, my kids had to watch what it was their parents always fast-forwarded through.

In this case it was an ad for Floam, little bags of multi-colored Styrofoam pellets that the shiny, happy commercial children used to make animals, balls, bike pads, and even sand castles indoors. With a bouncy song and quick cuts, the slick, hard-sell announcer worked his magic on my wide-eyed kids, who looked on, mouths agape in wonder, for the entire thirty seconds.

After a moment of silence my son spoke.

"We need to get some of that!"

"Can we, Daddy, can we get some?" his sister pleaded.

Where once there had been the thrill and satisfaction of watching a program on a lazy day, there now existed a void. A Floam-shaped hole opened up in my kids' hearts where just thirty seconds before there had been none. I knew I had to shut this down and quick.

"Sure," I said, "if you buy it with your own money. Do you want it enough to pay with your own dollars?" Turns out Floam was only worthy of *my* dollars, not *theirs*, saving me from hours of cleaning up little foam pellets for the next five years.

This is the world we live in—the world of more. And even though I was immune to Floam, my kids' particular weakness, I succumbed to my own version of more with my very own dollars, namely, guitar equipment. And it costs a whole lot more than Floam, I can tell you that!

The Floam-shaped void in our life is one only God can fill. He can teach us how to be content in Him without the need for more. He can show us how to be content no matter what we have or don't have if we'll let Him.

MORE IS LESS

In the middle of his existential rant about the meaning of life, Solomon turns his attention to this slippery concept of *more* (Ecclesiastes 6). In all his searching and wise evaluation of life, he's come across another grievous offense. People getting more and more of everything they crave in life, but winding up as nothings in the end. They get more but become less. He writes, "There is another serious tragedy I have seen under the sun, and it weighs heavily on humanity. God gives some people great wealth and honor and everything they could ever want, but then he doesn't give them the chance to enjoy these things. They die, and someone else, even a stranger, ends up enjoying their wealth! This is meaningless—a sickening tragedy" (Ecclesiastes 6:1–2).

In his example, a person gets everything they could ever want—money, fame, respect, and success. Yet they miss enjoyment, contentment, satisfaction, and fulfillment. This reminds us that the most important qualities we seek are not the result of what we have or don't have.

Some people have it all, says Solomon, but they might as well have nothing because none of it makes them happy. Solomon doesn't give the specifics of why these wealthy, successful people are not happy with their lives. He simply says, "God doesn't give them the chance," but I think it's easy to fill in the blanks. Notice that he says this tragedy "weighs heavy on humanity" (6:1). The phrase "weighs heavy" doesn't only mean it weighs us down; it can also mean that it "weighs on many," meaning, it's a prolific problem common to us all. And current studies back Solomon up.

Carol Graham is a researcher who studies happiness. As you can imagine, happiness is a difficult thing to measure, especially when comparing the results of different studies in different countries. Nevertheless, Graham discovered a curious reality: income does not guarantee happiness.

Surveys revealed happy and unhappy people in both rich and poor countries. In general, the richer the country, the greater the happiness, but plenty of poor countries had very high marks in happiness. The findings were so unexpected she gave the phenomenon a name: the "Happy Peasant and Miserable Millionaire" problem.

On the one hand, you have a peasant who reports that she is very happy. On the other hand, you have a wealthy CEO who reports she is miserable. Is it their expectations? Or maybe their natural dispositions?

Researchers struggle to explain this income-happiness disparity in objective ways, but they have found one definitive pattern. Humans have a remarkable ability to adapt to both prosperity and adversity. According to Graham, "The bottom line is that people can adapt to tremendous adversity and retain their natural cheerfulness, while they can also have virtually everything—including good health—and be miserable."[24]

ENOUGH ISN'T ENOUGH

This paradox sounds exactly like the "serious tragedy" Solomon described thousands of years earlier—people having everything and being unable to enjoy it. It's not a resource problem. It's a *contentment* problem.

Solomon goes on to describe a specific example of a man who has one hundred children and lives two thousand years. He may as well have said a trillion children and bazillion years because he's using a hyperbole. He wants you to know this guy has it all, more than you can wish for or imagine, but his fate is still a tragedy. He writes, "A man might have a hundred children and live to be very old. But if he finds no satisfaction in life and doesn't even get a decent burial, it would have been better for him to be born dead. His birth would have been meaningless, and he would have ended in darkness. He wouldn't even have had a name, and he would never have seen the sun or known of its existence. Yet he would have had more peace than in growing up to be an unhappy man. He might live a thousand years twice over but still not find contentment. And since he must die like everyone else—well, what's the use?" (Ecclesiastes 6:3–6).

We live in an individualistic society where personal achievement is how we attain status and legacy. Not so in Solomon's time. Children were a major status symbol of the ancient Hebrew culture. It was a family-centric culture, meaning, the bigger your family, the bigger your reputation, wealth, and legacy. You were your family, period. If you were the dad of a hundred children, then you must be quite the stud.

Imagine if one guy thought up every great invention of the last century—electricity, penicillin, space travel, the personal computer, the Internet, and to top it all off, coached the Dallas Cowboys to ten straight Super Bowl wins. That man would truly be the most incredible man in the world.

This is the type of man Solomon is describing. He's Einstein, da Vinci, Tom Landry, and Steve Jobs all rolled into one. This is the type of man, with all his inventions and accomplishments, that according to Solomon would be better off *not being born at all*. Say what? What makes a productive life of incredible accomplishment not worth living?

He didn't find any contentment.

According to Solomon, no matter what you do, buy, or achieve, if you don't find satisfaction, you're better off dead, because as soon as you finish one accomplishment, you'll be starving for the next. More leads to less until you are better off as nothing.

Did you notice in Solomon's example that the man didn't get a decent burial? A hundred kids and not one of them made sure Dad got sent off in honor and style. Could it be that he was so focused on producing child number one hundred, he ignored children one through ninety-nine? One of the more sinister problems with being addicted to more is that it makes us blind to what we have now.

Listen to what Solomon says in response to this story: "Enjoy what you have rather than desiring what you don't have. Just dreaming about nice things is meaningless—like chasing the wind" (Ecclesiastes 6:9).

I like the way one translation puts it: "Better is the sight of the eyes than the wandering of the appetite: this also is vanity and a striving after wind" (6:9, ESV). Notice how it highlights the distinction between what we can see (what we have in front of us) versus what we want (that which we do not have). Solomon's giving us one of the keys to contentment—seeing what you already have, not striving for what you don't have. God says "no" to the curse of more, but he says "yes" to the satisfaction of contentment.

THANKFULNESS COMPETITION

Have you ever been in a closed space with miserable, grumpy people? The negative energy seems to permeate everyone and soon people get nasty with each other. I had an experience like this in the car with my family. We were trying to go somewhere and do something fun, but the kids were grumping about it. Pretty soon I was grumping and my wife was, too. We were a rolling grouch-mobile of misery when suddenly, by the sheer undeserved grace of God, I had an idea.

"Thankfulness competition!" I yelled.

The rules were very simple. We would go around in a circle saying things we were thankful for. The first person who couldn't think of something, lost. My wife started, then I went, then the kids reticently joined in. After each response we cheered and clapped for the person who offered thanks, like they had swished a three-pointer from half-court. After a few rounds we were laughing and our moods had brightened. We were still on the way to do the same thing, but a brief focus on thankfulness transformed our grumpiness into contentment.

When we focus on the good things we already have, it changes us. It reminds us of how blessed we are and of all the things we take for granted. You have the chance to live in the wisdom of enjoying things while you have them, rather than lamenting when they are gone. You praise God for what you see rather than pray for what you want. It's like playing "I Spy" and listing all the individual items you're grateful for having instead of playing "Where's Waldo?" and looking for something elusive amid so much abundance. Thankfulness is key to contentment.

COMPARISON TRAP

On the other hand, comparison is the key to discontentment. Think about it: How do we find out about all the cool stuff we don't have? By seeing someone who does! This helps explain the Happy Peasant and Miserable Millionaire problem. The poor person only compares his life to other poor people and has no idea what he's missing.

The millionaire, however, is surrounded by, and inundated with, possessions and privileges beyond his reach. This compels him to focus on gaining equality with the people he envies. When you compare your worldly worth with someone who has more, your appetite trumps your eyes and robs you of contentment. It makes you blind to all your blessings. Immune to all you're worth.

This doesn't just happen to millionaires, of course, and the effect can be very subtle. It's that pull you feel every time you see someone with the updated version of your phone. It's the look you get from the valet attendant as you pull up in your nonluxury, dinged-up minivan. It's the pressure you feel every time you flip over the tag of the brand name jeans, gasping, and hoping your bank account can handle the load. It's the envy you experience when watching the big game at your neighbor's house on his new sixty-inch plasma flat-screen TV.

Comparison enflames our appetite and sparks our pride. It focuses our eyes on desiring what others have, rather than appreciating what we have. The best advice is to stop comparing yourself to others. And if it's too hard to stop comparing, then at least stop comparing up and start comparing down.

Don't get jealous of the thinner, lighter model of phone

that makes yours feel fatter and heavier. Compare down. Think of the guy that still uses the indestructible Nokia phone from ten years ago. Or think farther back to the days of the brick phone. At least you don't get a hernia every time the phone rings!

Instead of looking at all the luxury vehicles at the valet stand, look beyond them to the bus stop and be thankful for your car. Stand proud as you pass the keys over and tell them to watch out for the open wires sticking out of where your stereo used to be. Tell him you've counted the scratches and dents already so he better be careful and not add a new one.

And as you stand in front of your closet every morning, looking for something perfect to wear, take a look at the label that tells you where it was made. Think of those people living in a land you probably can't even find on a map, living lives you can't imagine, and consider how thankful they are just to have enough money to feed and clothe their family. And also remember, no matter how much those jeans cost today, some-day you *will* let them go for $2 at a garage sale.

The biggest thing we can do to find contentment is to re-place our want of more stuff with wanting more of God. Don't simply dampen your appetite; redirect that hunger to a relationship that brings lasting contentment.

UTS VERSUS OTS

One of the things we need to remember about Solomon is that he is often speaking from an under-the-sun perspective (UTS). He sees UTS people getting loads of UTS stuff and achieving all kinds of UTS accomplishments but still having no UTS satisfaction. It leads him to the conclusion that a UTS life has precious little to offer.

He gives some wise advice on how to be more content with your UTS life, namely "want what you have." His examples include enjoying your work, taking in a good meal, enjoying your spouse, and so on. I'll be honest, though. Even though it's good advice, these suggestions still sound like Band-Aids. It's like when I tell my kids, "It's okay—you'll get through this" when they don't make the cut for something at school. It's like handing a hungry person an invitation to your church. It's a nice gesture, but their stomach is still rumbling.

Earlier Solomon reminds us that God "has planted eternity in the human heart…" (Ecclesiastes 3:11). Our under-the-sun hearts have a taste for over-the-sun things. Why do people who have so much constantly crave *more*? Because the over-the-sun (OTS) desires of our hearts can only be satisfied with over-the-sun things. Or as C. S. Lewis famously said, "If I find in myself a desire which no experience in this world can satisfy, the most probable explanation is that I was made for another world."[25]

The only healthy expression of our insatiable desire for more is to desire more of God. When we get this one desire straight, when we seek OTS things to satisfy OTS needs, we finally find contentment in all the UTS stuff as well.

When people burn all their bridges and forsake everyone who loves them to achieve UTS things such as promotions, status, and money, it is often to feed the OTS desire for approval. The answer isn't found in more achievements or recognition; it's found in more of God.

When people max out credit cards buying stuff they can't

afford to project an image they can never live up to, they're trying to buy the OTS gift of acceptance with UTS stuff. They don't need a brand-new look; they need more of God.

When people stash away cash in savings accounts and buy a dozen different types of insurance policies, have their doctor on speed dial, and drive all the people they love crazy with overbearing concern, they're trying to buy the OTS gift of security with UTS things. They don't need to be more vigilant; they need more of God.

There's nothing inherently wrong with working hard and reaching goals. Having nice things and taking care of them are not sins. Wanting the best for those you love and working hard to protect them are good things. But all these UTS things are done in vain if you have no regard for your OTS desires and your OTS God.

Solomon was well accomplished at building his own kingdom. In fact, he describes some of his building efforts earlier in Ecclesiastes. Several commentators have pointed out that the king refers to himself more than ten times in describing his accomplishments by using phrases like, "for myself," "I built," and "I bought," without a single mention of God (2:4–10). Even though he had a close relationship with God as a youth and was king over God's chosen people, when it came time to build a kingdom, Solomon built his own and built it his way. As he focused on making and getting more, he had less and less.

We don't have the resources of Solomon, but if we take whatever we have and marshal it to serve the Kingdom of Me rather than the Kingdom of God, we wind up in the same place. When you build your own kingdom, the curse of wanting more kicks in. You become a fat cat with fewer and fewer options, less and less mobility, and ever-diminishing contentment. Your more becomes less until you feel like you have nothing at all.

It doesn't have to be this way. When we build God's Kingdom, when we seek His friendship and values every day, arranging all of our resources in the service of His Kingdom, our weaknesses become strengths and what little we have becomes more. Exponentially more.

This kingdom growth is the more that leads to more. It is also the more that leads to contentment, because as you find your purpose, identity, and resources in God, you find yourself blessed with what Solomon so desperately lacked in all his wealth and accomplishment: the ability to enjoy it.

We don't need more stuff or accomplishment; we need more of God. And when we seek Him and spend our time and resources building His kingdom with His power, we find that God says a hearty "Yes!" to our contentment.

LEARNING CONTENTMENT

We see this kind of divine contentment in Paul, who said he "learned how to be content with whatever I have" (Philippians 4:11). This didn't just happen—he was not simply born with a disposition to be content; he had to *learn* it. Contentment is not a magic disposition that falls out of heaven; it is something we experience as we grow and mature in our knowledge of God and our practice of faith.

Paul says that living with contentment is a secret or mystery: "I know how to live on almost nothing or with everything. I have learned the *secret* of living in every situation, whether it is with a full stomach or empty, with plenty or little" (Philippians 4:12).

The phrase "I have learned" could literally be translated "I have been initiated," and it points to a knowledge that was previously unknown but has now been revealed. People everywhere today are looking for contentment, just as they were in Paul's day. Being initiated into living with contentment is an art that requires effort, discipline, and an awareness of who we are and whose we are. It is amazing how much can change in our lives when we get intentional about learning to live with contentment.

Paul continues to reveal where the secret of contentment lies for a Christian: "For I can do everything through Christ who gives me strength" (Philippians 4:13). We see this verse painted under the eyes of college football players or on the uniforms of professional boxers. But notice that the context of the verse isn't sports or achievement, but it is contentment and specifically contentment in economic hardships. Have you ever thought about how this verse applies to your bank account? Your mortgage balance? Your credit card? No matter what your account balances are, you can do everything through Christ. Paul learned to rest in what God does or doesn't provide, to trust Him when we go without, and to realize this, too, is a blessing from God.

Contentment isn't sustained from the outside in, but from the inside out. It is primarily a matter of the heart. Some people look content on the outside, but inside their minds are full of turmoil. *Contentment is a quieting of the mind before God.* We submit to His work and His sovereignty in our lives.

This doesn't imply that we don't share our frustrations with God or with friends, but we are careful not to cross over into grumbling against God and whining about our situation. We bear it under His grace and we do it freely. It is not that we must be content, but that we willingly yield to God and are *freely content* even in our trials. We take pleasure in the working of His will and situations in our life. We trust Him in everything, even when we don't understand His ways.

To unpack the mystery of contentment, I drew on one of my favorite sources, *The Rare Jewel of Christian Contentment*, a devotional classic by seventeenth-century English pastor Jeremiah Burroughs in which he shares some surprising insights. The Christian is "the most contented man in the world," he writes, "and yet the most unsatisfied man in the world."[26] What he means is that we are content in God and what He provides, but we are never satisfied with anything less than God. We enjoy what God provides, but our ultimate contentment is in God Himself. We are thankful for health, peace, relationships, and work, but it is never enough. We *must* have the God of our health, peace, relationships, and work, or it will not satisfy.

We come "to contentment, not so much by way of addition," Burroughs argues, "but by way of subtraction."[27] In our culture the way to achieve contentment is to add things to our possessions or circumstances, but for a Christian we can lower or subtract our desires to accommodate our possessions. No matter what our condition, we thank God and trust He is working for the best in our lives. We have what we have from the very hand of God so who are we to keep demanding more and looking past what God is doing in us?

A believer comes "to contentment, not so much by getting

rid of the burden that is on him," says Burroughs, but "by adding another burden to himself."[28] Rather than spending all our effort bemoaning the affliction we are enduring, we should be more burdened with our selfishness and sin. By humbling ourselves before God and seeing His grace and mercy, we experience the joy of forgiveness and a relationship with God. We remember that if we really got what we deserved in life, we'd end up broken and lost.

After all, the Bible teaches what we really deserve for our sin is hell and God is good enough to provide another way. So we become "poor in spirit," as Jesus reminds us (Matthew 5:3). We remember our sin that separates us from God and focus more on living each day in His love than on what we don't have. This shifts our thinking back to God and the daily miracle of His grace.

Burroughs reminds us that one can arrive at this contentment "not by making up the wants of his circumstances, but by the performance of the work of his circumstances."[29] We get busy doing the work that God has called us to in the situation we find ourselves in. Sure, we may not have chosen these circumstances, but we can go about serving God in the midst of them and find contentment there.

Often in our culture if something is taken away, money or a career path, we strive as if we can never be content until we get the money or career back. But learning contentment implies that we accept our circumstances as from God and strive to serve Him faithfully no matter the situation. Burroughs says a believer "enjoys much of God in everything he has, and knows how to make up all wants in God himself."[30] This is the lifelong journey of learning the art of contentment.

Chapter Eight

Yes to Wisdom

If you prize wisdom, she will make you great. Embrace her, and she will honor you.

—*Proverbs 4:8*

Years ago some mysterious wreckage allegedly appeared on an Arizona highway. The charred metal fragments resembled an airplane crash, but also included some familiar car parts—tires, bumpers, hood, and windshield. It took a while for investigators to piece together what happened.

An Air Force sergeant had somehow got hold of a Jet Assisted Take-Off Unit (JATO) and decided to scratch his inventor's itch by strapping it to his old 1967 Chevy Impala. JATO units are solid fuel rockets used to give heavy military transport airplanes an extra push for takeoff from short airfields. Consequently, when he ignited the JATO unit, his rocket-fueled Chevy quickly reached a speed of 250 mph!

His Chevy traveled 2.6 miles in fifteen seconds, at which

point the would-be inventor applied the brakes, completely melting them and blowing the tires. Then the Impala *left* the ground and rocketed an additional 1.3 miles, directly into a cliff 125 feet above the road, leaving a three-foot-deep, blackened crater in the rock. A thrilling ride, but not the way anyone wants to leave this earth.

This story was so horrible, yet so funny, and such a perfect example of utter foolishness, it launched a tongue-in-cheek awards society known as the Darwin Awards. Their mission is to "salute the improvement of the human genome by honoring those who accidentally remove themselves from it."

Since 1995, the Darwin Awards have officially collected, verified, and graded the stupidest ways people have unintentionally ended their lives. The great irony of the Darwin Awards is the story that started it all has been proven to be false. The JATO car is an urban myth, debunked by the Arizona Highway Patrol, and disproven by the guys on *Mythbusters*. No person was ever so foolish to die in a 250 mph airborne jet-car, but there's been plenty of sensational foolishness to keep the site running to this day. In all, the website has given out nearly four hundred awards.

Foolishness is in great supply. Wisdom is a little harder to find. And I don't have to judge the Darwin Awards to realize how foolish people can be—I just look at my own life. While I hope I never win a Darwin, I've still learned my share of lessons the hard way.

In high school I struggled with Algebra I, but rather than work hard and learn the material, I decided to take a shortcut. Our teacher was advanced in his years and becoming a little senile. He would often leave his grade book open on his desk when he needed to step out of the room. One day near the end of the semester, I made my way up and looked at my name and noticed there were no grades recorded because I had turned in no homework. So I took a pencil and gave myself all A's! It actually worked until I tried to do it again in Algebra II, flunked, and had to spend all summer in summer school while everyone else had fun.

Or the time I impulsively bought a used pickup truck with hardly any money down and over 17 percent interest. It almost pulled me under trying to make the payments, but it was worth it considering what I learned about debt and impulses. I could go on, but we all know what it is like to mess up. Wouldn't it be great if we could gain insight that was tried and tested over thousands of years, that was inspired by God Himself, that would give us principles to avoid many of these kinds of mistakes in life? Thankfully, the Bible is full of wisdom, both in Proverbs and in Ecclesiastes. We only have to be wise enough to use it. Saying yes to God means saying yes to living with His wisdom.

DON'T BE AN IDIOT

Solomon was considered the most supernaturally wise and knowledgeable man who has ever lived. A king consulted by rulers from all over the world, he regularly doled out advice in exchange for riches. He wrote much of the book of Proverbs, providing wisdom in simple couplets comparing one thing to another, a wise thing to a foolish thing. From the opening chapters of Ecclesiastes, Solomon doesn't really come across as this world-wise sage. However, in Chapter 7, the teacher of timeless wisdom finally emerges, serving up truth like the royal wise guy he was known to be.

He lays out some super-concentrated, ultra-refined advice for getting the most out of life. He talks of the importance of character, the refining value of sorrow, and the power of our own mortality to focus our attention on what matters most. He encourages people to finish what they start, to control their temper, and not to pine away for the past. He reminds people that money is powerful, God is in control, and nothing is certain.

Several times he's mentioned pursuing wisdom in his quest for significance, but this was the best of human thinking "under the sun." He already declared earlier in his life that this would be a failure because true wisdom begins with God. "The fear of the LORD is the beginning of wisdom, and knowledge of the Holy One is understanding" (Proverbs 9:10, NIV). This fear doesn't mean we walk around in terror, cringing every time we think of God. It simply means that we revere and respect Him and His laws. The foundational aspect of wisdom, where the life of wisdom really begins, is not with a college degree, but with faith and respect for the God who created us.

Solomon's proverbs in Ecclesiastes ring like much of the other wisdom he shared: very plain to see, very easy to understand, and very challenging to do. This blend of absorption and application, taking in and acting on the wisdom handed to us by others, is crucial to a fulfilling life. In fact, our word "idiot" comes from the Greek word *idios*, which doesn't mean "stupid" or "ignorant," but just "of oneself." It would be like a tradesman who never learned the right and proper way to do his job, someone who started working without any kind of apprenticeship. This person does it on his own and qualifies as an *idios*. In contrast, wisdom is like a master craftsman who comes alongside us with lessons to build a well-made life.

"Wisdom is supreme; therefore get wisdom," we're told in Proverbs. "Though it cost all you have, get understanding" (4:7). Most of us learn the hard way that real wisdom should not be confused with knowledge or our intelligence level. Living wisely has little to do with your IQ, SAT score, or college degree. Wisdom, as the Bible defines it, centers on learning how to live rather than how much we know. You can have a Ph.D. and not be wise according to biblical standards. Or you can be a high school dropout and grow to be very wise.

Historian and journalist Paul Johnson points out the difference in his book *Intellectuals*. He looks at the moral decisions many of the key thinkers of modern times made in their lives. From Jean Jacques Rousseau to philosopher Jean Paul Sartre to Ernest Hemingway, Leo Tolstoy, Karl Marx, and Bertrand Russell. In chapter after chapter he chronicles their mistakes, arrogance, and instability. They are living proof that intelligence is not the same thing as wisdom.

Rousseau, who had great influence in his writing on the modern theory of the education of children that still shapes culture today, *abandoned* five of his kids to an orphanage. None of his kids were even given names, just dropped off on the steps, essentially so that their mother could take care of Rousseau completely without distractions. Based on the survival rate of children in these institutions, most of them likely died.[31] The only woman he claimed to really love, Sophie d'Houdetot, said of him years after his death, "He was ugly enough to frighten me and love did not make him more attractive. But he was a pathetic figure and I treated him with gentleness and kindness. He was an interesting madman."[32]

Karl Marx, the revolutionary philosopher behind communism and socialism who has shaped the ideas of political figures around the world, was personally unwilling to work, a horrible manager of money, and a person filled with anger and bitterness. Paul Johnson suggests that his whole vision for a communist economic structure may have been as much about his inability to handle money as anything. Most disturbing is the suggestion that for all his writing about the working class, he really didn't know anybody from the working class very well, other than their family's maid. Marx never paid the maid a dime other than giving her room and board, despite all his writing on fair wages. He did, however, father an illegitimate child with her, whom he refused to admit was his and only formally met once, though the young man did not know Marx was his father at the time.

Jean Paul Sartre, who popularized existentialism and the idea that all of life comes down to individual freedom and choice, was embraced as a spiritual leader by hundreds of thousands, if not millions, of people in the last century. While he was often revolutionary in his ideas and writings, he actually did very little in politics outside of producing words. During World War II, he did almost nothing for the Resistance and zero to save or protect the Jews. He gave his attention to furthering his career by writing plays, novels, and treatises on philosophy.[33] He treated his lover, Simone de Beauvoir, unfaithfully and usually had one or more other mistresses in his life. He viewed women as commodities to possess and conquer.

There is no question that these individuals were brilliant thinkers and writers, but by biblical standards they emerge as fools. They were not living with wisdom. As Paul Johnson summarized: "One of the principal lessons of our tragic century, which has seen so many millions of innocent lives sacrificed in schemes to improve the lot of humanity, is—beware intellectuals. Not merely should they be kept well away from the levers of power, they should also be objects of particular suspicion when they seek to offer collective advice."[34]

Wisdom is not about how much you know, but how you live. Biblical wisdom helps us understand the meaning of life and how life works. These principles apply to everyone and reflect timeless wisdom about God, human nature, relationships, and much more. Proverbs are not promises or a magic formula but simply a distillation of truth that can show us the wisdom of God in the daily details of our lives.

THE VOICE OF WISDOM

Have you noticed how many TV commercials have attractive women selling their products? Maybe there's a precedent for this approach that has nothing to do with sex appeal. In Proverbs, Solomon describes wisdom as a woman raising her voice in public to share the truth with those around her. "Listen as Wisdom calls out! Hear as understanding raises her voice! On the hilltop along the road, she takes her stand at the crossroads. By the gates at the entrance to the town, on the road leading in, she cries aloud, 'I call to you, to all of you! I raise my voice to all people. You simple people, use good judgment. You foolish people, show some understanding. Listen to me! For I have important things to tell you'" (Proverbs 8:1–6).

This is far different from the typical personification of wisdom as a quiet guru or ancient hermit dispensing his truth from a distant mountaintop. The wisdom described in Proverbs 8 is loud. She calls out and raises her voice, eager to be heard. Wisdom is also prominent and stands around very noticeable places. She shouts at people in the places where they find themselves most often.

And wisdom is right without being arrogant or unduly self-righteous. The word used most often for "wisdom" in the original language of Scripture doesn't merely mean "correct." It carries the idea of a "peaceful arrangement." Wisdom is so true, so correct, that she sorts your jumbled thoughts into a peaceful order. God is not a God of confusion but of order and a sound mind.

Lastly, wisdom is clear. She's not hard to understand and doesn't speak in riddles. The only thing she's selling is the truth we so desperately need to hear and act on in our lives. And like any good sales pitch, she includes not only the benefits of wisdom but what we need to do to obtain them. She not only lists what she has to offer—riches, success, common sense, insight—she emphatically calls people to four actions to release the power of wisdom in their lives: search, listen, choose, and follow.

Searching for wisdom is easy. It's readily available if we're willing to look for it and receive it. In Solomon's description, wisdom promises to be found by all who seek her. James mentions the ready availability of wisdom as well, always given to those who ask (James 1:5).

The problems start in the listening, choosing, and following areas. In Proverbs 8, wisdom implores people to listen four separate times, like a parent trying to get their reluctant, distracted kids to do their homework. She practically has to shout until she's blue in the face!

Choosing and following wisdom are big stumbling blocks as well. At least they are for me. I don't have a problem finding wisdom; I have a problem following it. I'm too content to be a biblical idiot, stuck in my own little world, doing things my way, and ignoring wisdom's life-straightening advice.

I know certain foods are bad for me, but I eat them anyway. I know I should read an enlightening book, but it's so much easier to watch mindless TV. I know I should wait and cool off before I hit the send button, but instead I don't hesitate to flame someone that angered me. There is no shortage of wisdom, just a shortage of me responding. Wisdom can't guide us if emotions hijack our hearts, and Solomon was well aware of this common occurrence.

HERE COMES THE BRIBE

Wisdom, from a biblical perspective, offers much more insight into living than our most respected leaders and admired celebrities can provide. I noticed this especially when I came across a popular book entitled, of all things, *Wisdom*. Author and photographer Andrew Zuckerman traveled the world and conducted over fifty interviews with some of the most accomplished and renowned figures in politics, art, music, filmmaking, writing, sports, and acting, each one over the age of sixty-five.

From Clint Eastwood to Nelson Mandela, from Vanessa Redgrave to Yoko Ono, he asked them questions about work, love, conflict, and the environment. Zuckerman's true purpose, however, the thing he was really hoping to walk away with, wasn't mere answers to common problems. He was chasing down wisdom.

The result was his book *Wisdom*, which then hit bookstores with the kinds of accolades and media coverage you might expect from such a star-studded, high-profile project. People were thrilled by this amazing opportunity to soak up the filtered, concentrated life experience of these highly accomplished, seasoned people.

But as I was reading the book, it didn't take me long to get fatigued. Though long on wonderful stories, personal epiphanies, and everyday observations, it seemed oddly short on wisdom. In fact, I got the sense that many of the people interviewed didn't feel comfortable as vessels of wisdom. Several had trouble even defining what wisdom was, and often rambled on about things that were merely interesting or true. The most troubling thing of all was how many words were on each page. Wisdom usually isn't so verbose, running down bunny trails, turning back on itself, and fizzling out, as many of their statements seemed to do.

In fact, Solomon doles out more wisdom in a few verses than this entire book of celebrity interviews. Each one of his insights is concise and direct and resonates in obvious as well as profound ways. For example, right in the middle of fourteen verses of proverbs on wisdom, Solomon writes, "Extortion turns wise people into fools, and bribes corrupt the heart" (Ecclesiastes 7:7). Now, I tend to skip over proverbs on bribery because I imagine some sleazy government official sliding a bundle of cash into his cloak with an evil sneer and wicked grin. I've never taken a cash bribe or extorted anything from anybody. I figure verses like this one apply only to government leaders and people in power, reminding them of the pitfalls of abusing their authority.

Then I started thinking about what a bribe is. It's a situation where a decision maker chooses to benefit themselves rather than the people or purpose they serve. They choose an immediate benefit (cash, privilege, indebtedness) rather than doing what's right. It not only compromises their character, but makes a person into a fool. I'm convinced that whenever wisdom calls for action, we can expect a bribe tempting us to compromise not far behind.

This is how we can be surrounded by wisdom that is so easy to find and understand but still feel so lost. We hear wisdom's voice, but something comes along and bribes us, offering a short-term benefit that ultimately makes us into fools. Our desires act like extortionists, bypassing wisdom to get whatever we want.

Too many married people have taken a bribe of self-esteem or sensual gratification, getting sexually involved with someone who is not their spouse, only to have it cost them everything they truly value. We say, how could he be so foolish? Why would she throw away all she has? Bribes corrupt the heart.

Or consider the person who ignores family, relationships,

and even their own health in order to focus on a career that can never love them back or provide lasting satisfaction. They wind up alone, empty, and broken. How did someone so smart and so successful win at business but fail at significance? Extortion makes a would-be wise man into a fool. All you hear is the desperate voice of brokenness crying, "You must succeed at all costs," unable to hear the call of wisdom, which asks, "What does true success look like? What does it matter if you gain the world but lose your soul?"

It's the student who knows how destructive drugs are and the kind of people who will be at the party, but goes anyway. They ignore wisdom and accept a bribe to feel popular. The extorting voice of acceptance makes it impossible to hear the depth of biblical wisdom when it says, "Bad company corrupts good character" (1 Corinthians 15:33).

Solomon isn't just talking about a handful of bureaucrats when he warns of the wisdom-destroying power of bribery and extortion. He was talking to all of us. Want to be wise? Search, listen, choose, and follow. Want to remain wise? Refuse the bribes. Stop extorting. Don't let your emotions and desires short-circuit wisdom's power in your life. Don't let some temporary benefit or powerful urge disrupt the peaceful arrangement that wisdom brings.

WISE UP

The Psalmist writes, "Joyful are people of integrity, who follow the instructions of the Lord. Joyful are those who obey his laws and search for him with all their hearts" (Psalm 119:1–2). When we walk in the ways of God and follow His instructions, the result is joy beyond measure. If you want to wise up, lean into these recommendations and reminders distilled from Solomon's experiences.

Live Honorably

Solomon says, "A good reputation is more valuable than costly perfume" (Ecclesiastes 7:1). Perfume was very costly in the ancient world, but Solomon points to the greater value of a good reputation. One's reputation over the long haul is rooted in one's character.

Your amazing looks and great personality may eventually get you married, but it is your character and integrity that will keep you married. Your gifts and abilities may open career doors for you, but your character and integrity will ensure you're successful in that career over the long haul. God may have given you the gift of children, but your character and integrity will determine your ability to influence and communicate with your kids.

Your character determines how far you go and whether you like yourself when you get there. A person of character manages the small decisions for longer-term impact. As Ralph Waldo Emerson said, "The force of character is cumulative." Each day we are building a life, a career, a reputation by the choices we make. It may not always be visible to others, but eventually it will be. I mean, let's face it, nobody wakes up and decides to tank their lives and careers because of integrity issues. We don't make an entry in our diary one day: "Dear Diary, today I plan to commit fraud, which will eventually lead to the demise of my career, a nervous breakdown, and ultimately jail." Character drifts subtly and slowly, eroding in small choices over time.

One way we can manage the small decisions is to live by a basic media mode of operation: refrain from doing anything in private we'd be uncomfortable posting on Facebook, reading about in tomorrow's headlines, or being recorded for eternity on YouTube.

Remember the End

Solomon says, "A wise person thinks a lot about death, while a fool thinks only about having a good time" (Ecclesiastes 7:4). Confronting our own mortality is difficult. We'd rather not think about it, say YOLO, and move on, but wisdom urges us to be aware of our own mortality.

This reality drives us to inject purpose into every moment and cherish every relationship. The people who are most aware of their mortality tend to spend their lives most richly. Foolish people take the bribe that there is no end, death isn't worth thinking about, and the point of life is to amuse themselves to death.

Receive Criticism Well

Solomon continues, "Better to be criticized by a wise person than to be praised by a fool" (Ecclesiastes 7:5). At one point a wise and gutsy coworker came to me and confronted me about my pride. He claimed I was no longer listening to the people around me. I was not treating their ideas with respect. I had stopped learning and growing as a person and this was apparent to my coworkers. I had allowed pride to slip into my heart in a negative way.

I responded to this person with maturity, something like, "Who do you think you are to walk into my office and accuse me of being arrogant?" After the dust settled from the explosion of my ego, it really hurt to realize this person was right. Later, I thanked my coworker for having the guts to call me out. Now don't get me wrong in all this. A person can be self-assured and confident. That's way different from allowing pride to blind us and not treating others with respect.

No one likes to hear they screwed up. No one likes to find out they have massive room for improvement. It's much nicer, much more comfortable, to continue on in the assumption that we are just fine the way we are. When someone like a parent, a boss, or a mentor sits us down and shares hard truths about our character and conduct, foolishness comes along with a bribe saying, "You're fine, no need to listen, they have no idea what they're talking about." All your foolish friends will be right there to defend you, but all they care about is who you are rather than what you could be. Don't take that bribe. Take heart and press on. Choose wisdom.

Finish Well

"Finishing is better than starting," says Solomon and concludes, "Patience is better than pride" (Ecclesiastes 7:8). Your first steps in the right direction may be difficult, but you gain momentum with each wise choice you make. Others may be going a different direction or encouraging you to follow them and their advice. But we must stick to what is true—about

God, about ourselves, and about what He calls us to do with our lives.

Whether they credit God or not, most successful people learn the art of finishing well. After actor Harrison Ford's first performance as a hotel bellhop in the film *Dead Heat on a Merry-Go-Round*, a Columbia executive called him into his office. "Sit down, kid," the executive said. After a few words he dismissed him with, "You ain't got it, kid, you ain't got it...." His movies have gone on to gross billions. It's never about how you start, ultimately, but how you finish.[35]

Anybody can start something. We start the diet, workout regimen, hobby, or planning, but it takes persistence, work, effort, and discipline to see it through. It will take patience as well because one key rule about being good at anything is first you have to be willing to be bad at it, often for a long time!

Temper Control

"Control your temper," Ecclesiastes continues, "for anger labels you a fool" (7:9). Think of the anger spectrum. On one end of the spectrum are hotheads who get angry too easily or at the wrong things, in the wrong ways. It's like the Incredible Hulk. This guy can lose his cool over any number of things and he becomes green, his clothes rip, and he goes out-of-control nuts.

On the other end of the spectrum you've got Ned Flanders from *The Simpsons*. Ned Flanders is the father of a devoutly Christian family and is often used as a caricature of Christians. Ned is nice, very nice, so nice that he seems like a wimp. He seems naïve and weak; he is not respected and his words carry no weight at all. He never gets angry.

Ned is the opposite of the Hulk and doesn't get angry easily enough! Wisdom tells us to control our anger, not pretend it's not there. Too many Neds of the world are passive and indifferent about things that really matter. There are some things that we all should be angry about—sin, rape, murder, racism, terrorism, poverty, child abuse, human trafficking, etc. Some things are just plain evil. God hates them and they make Him angry. Things like this should rightfully make you angry, too. If a person looks at sin and doesn't get angry, something is wrong.

In between the hotheads and the Neds, we find the anger of Jesus, who represents the heart and character of God. We can call this righteous anger. The goal is not to get rid of anger altogether. What grieves God should grieve us. What maddens God should madden us. We want to deal with anger issues in a healthy way and especially be aware of the unhealthy and foolish anger in all of us.

There is always a price when our anger is not dealt with in a healthy way. Psychologist Raymond Novaco found that suppressed anger has many of the same negative cardiovascular health consequences as expressed anger![36] Studies have suggested that suppressed anger has the power to shorten your life and affect your health in a significant way.

One study shows that the angrier we become, the more certain we are about our judgments. When we are angry, we "know" we are right. And that's a huge potential leadership fault, considering how emotions can mess up our ability to think rationally. Explode frequently enough, publicly

enough, and no matter how good and kind you are 99 percent of the time, that 1 percent will define you and brand you
as an intolerable fool.

Don't take the bribe.

A DIVIDED HEART

As we've seen, even Solomon wasn't immune to bribery and
extortion. I don't know if he ever accepted money in exchange
for a court ruling or a government contract, but he absolutely
cashed in the wisdom of God for his own idiocy. The Bible
summarizes it for us in: "Now King Solomon loved many foreign women.... The LORD had clearly instructed the people
of Israel, 'You must not marry them, because they will turn
your hearts to their gods.' Yet Solomon insisted on loving
them anyway" (1 Kings 11:1–2).

God had blessed Solomon with supernatural wisdom,
which made the king rich and successful beyond measure. He
was the son of a man who followed God with all of his heart.
Solomon had every advantage imaginable, but the world's
wisest man was an idiot when it came to women. Rather than
following the Lord's commands and letting the Lord establish
His kingdom, Solomon took a bribe: here's sexual satisfaction
as well as political stability if you just ignore that minor stip-
ulation of only taking Israelite wives. Perhaps he considered
the spirit of the law, foreign women turning his heart away
from God, and thought, "There's no way that can happen to
the wisest man alive!"

One verse later it has. And in fact, they did turn his
heart away from God: "In Solomon's old age, they turned

his heart to worship other gods instead of being completely faithful to the LORD his God, as his father, David, had been" (1 Kings 11:4).

He took what he wanted instead of doing what the law required. The gift of wisdom was still in effect in Solomon's life, but the gift of God's relationship grew more and more distant. In his old age, the time when he wrote the wise words of Ecclesiastes, Solomon's heart seems to be coming back to God after being divided among a thousand women and their many gods. His lack of respect for God's laws sent Israel into a civil war that resulted in a divided kingdom.

We can all drift subtly into this kind of a life. We can all begin to bypass wisdom for foolishness, eternal perspectives for immediate gratification, and the big picture for shortsightedness. It's a choice we must make every day, in small choices and in large ones. Wisdom requires discernment, and the best way to discern what's true is to stay connected to the source of Truth—God.

Chapter Nine
Yes to Heaven

To go to heaven, fully to enjoy God, is infinitely
better than the most pleasant accommodations
here.

—Jonathan Edwards

A large, brown, and battered cardboard box arrived in the
mail. I didn't give much thought as to what might be in it
before I opened it up and peered inside. Immediately, tears
welled up in my eyes. My siblings had sent me the last items
from my dad's estate that they thought I might want after he
had passed away earlier in the year. I had a great relationship
with my dad, and I respected him and looked up to him completely. He was a mentor to me and someone I turned to for
wisdom whenever I needed it.

I pulled out the item on top—a miniature Dallas Cowboys
football helmet I'd had signed for him. He was a devoted
Cowboys fan. It simply said, "To Carlos, Michael Irvin." I remember how excited I was when I met Michael Irvin and had

him sign it, and I recalled my phone conversation from my dad when he received it.

Memories of him flooded me—going out with him as a kid to fly remote-controlled model airplanes that he loved to build, the countless hours we'd spent together remodeling our first house, a definite fixer-upper Lori and I had purchased, and the many conversations and laughs. I thought about his smile. And then I lost it. The fact that I couldn't just pick up the phone and talk to him, couldn't hop on a plane and see him, flooded me in a huge wave of grief. I sat there a long time with that little helmet and said through my tears, "I miss you, Dad."

In that moment, however, something beautiful transpired: hope bloomed. I thought about heaven and the reality that there is more beyond this life. I wiped away my tears, smiled, and continued, "I look forward to seeing you again soon." I was grieving, but as someone with a very real hope.

GOOD GRIEF

Losing someone you love is one of the hardest realities of life. The emotions hit you in the most random of times. For me they can be seeing a young man help his father out of the car in a parking lot, hearing a lyric in a song that suddenly seems strangely poignant, seeing a birthday reminder pop up on my calendar that I never deleted, or eating a familiar food. You wish more than anything that you could get back lost time, that you could see that loved one again, hear them laugh, see them smile. But you can't.

The all-consuming reality of death is yet another tragedy

Solomon finds under the sun. He writes of the universal nature of death and notes that, "It seems so tragic that everyone
under the sun suffers the same fate. That is why people are
not more careful to be good. Instead, they choose their own
mad course, for they have no hope. There is nothing ahead
but death anyway. There is hope only for the living. As they
say, 'It's better to be a live dog than a dead lion!'" (Ecclesiastes: 9:3–4).

Once again Solomon takes a long, hard look at life. The
king sees a variety of people, some who are wise, upright,
good, and religious, and others who are foolish, wicked, bad,
and godless. Humanity is complicated and varied. It is full
of unique individuals populating a vast spectrum that ranges
from very good to horribly bad, but Solomon sees one unit-
ing reality among them all—everybody dies.

In fact, the Hebrew word he uses for "tragedy" is normally
translated as "evil." The primary meaning is the "absence of
all good," but it can also carry the idea of "hindering or sev-
ering a relationship to a person or principle which is proper."
In other words, death just doesn't seem right. It severs something that shouldn't be severed. Death is a "natural" process
that feels completely unnatural. Better to be a live dog than a
dead lion, he concludes. The lion was a highly esteemed animal and was used as the insignia of the house of David, but
dogs were seen as lowly and disgusting animals. Solomon sees
no good in death here. It's the terrible equalizer—no one escapes it. It's tragic, and hope seems to slip through his fingers
like sand.

But when we say yes to God, it impacts our view of life
now and life beyond right now. We have the hope of heaven

to look forward to, a real hope based on the promise of God's Word. We don't have to despair nor do we have to put our stock in the material things of this world. We have hope in Christ for living joyously in harmony with God forever.

THE ODDS OF HOPE

Researchers have found that human beings on the whole are optimistic. One recent study in the *Journal of Experimental Psychology* confirmed this theory by asking football fans to predict the outcomes of upcoming games. Participants were given access to point-spread data and motivated with cash rewards to pick winners. Even though there was clear data to let them know which was the superior team, a predictable trend developed. People in the study picked their favorite teams to win, no matter what, even if they were obviously inferior. On average, four out of five people expected their favorite team to win regardless of the odds.[37]

This hardwired optimism surfaces in all aspects of life, from purchases to relationships and health. A wellspring of hope flows through all our choices, calling us forward through life. We tend to feel things will work out well for us, no matter what current evidence might reveal.

This can be an incredibly positive quality, especially when striving to meet important goals. Hope allows us to look past setbacks and suffering and strain toward an objective. Psychologists also point out that optimism can lead to negative results, such as people refusing to go to the doctor because "everything will work out just fine," or someone spending the precious few dollars they have on lottery tickets, because "they know this one's a winner."

Regardless of whether the outcome of optimism is good or bad, studies confirm what most know from personal experience—humans are hardwired for hope. When that hope is gone, our lives fall apart. Especially when we have no ultimate hope. Solomon observed this firsthand and notes the results: "That is why people are not more careful to be good. Instead, they choose their own mad course, for they have no hope. There is nothing ahead but death anyway. There is hope only for the living" (Ecclesiastes 9:3).

The ancient Hebrew concept of the afterlife was fairly undefined. Most experts agree that people in Solomon's day believed the dead went to a place called *Sheol*, which is another word for "the grave." Although it's a general reference for death, Sheol came to be known as an actual location under the surface of the earth. In either case, once you went to Sheol, you were forgotten on earth and never returned.

So here's our guy Solomon, supernaturally gifted with wisdom. Most people probably coasted through the endless activity of life on the wings of their natural optimism, not even thinking too much about death, but not Solomon. He couldn't help but observe the utter futility and agony of living in a heavenless world. If there's no reward for good living, no relief to this hard life, what's the point in being decent? What's the point in being born at all? The only advice he offers is to enjoy the simple pleasures of life. And while food, drink, and relationships can be rich sources of satisfaction, they ultimately can't provide the kind of hope one can build an eternity on. As humans, we need something more. We need the security of knowing what's next after our life on earth has ended.

The irony is that many modern philosophies eschew the concept of heaven as childish and harmful. The thinking is that people who cling to promises of the afterlife don't make the most of their time on earth. It's the idea that religion is a crutch and only makes humans weak and dependent on something intangible and possibly nonexistent. It's also the basis for schools of thought such as humanism, which encourages people to take responsibility for their lives and enjoy every moment as they do what they want to do.

It can even slide into hedonism in which the emphasis is on just "going for the gusto" and enjoying all the sensual pleasures of this life since that's all we have. On the other end of the spectrum, existentialists encourage people to embrace the fact that this life is all we have and take responsibility for their choices. While some find this kind of burden liberating, many people find it bleak and depressing.

Secular thinkers have claimed for decades that the false promise of heaven makes people bad citizens of earth. Since rewards await them in the afterlife, adherents fail to make this world any better. It's a sentiment found in John Lennon's famous song "Imagine." The song is incredibly emotive. In his voice you feel the longing for a better, more illuminated world. In Ecclesiastes 9, Solomon says, in essence: "I don't have to imagine it, I'm living it! I am surrounded by people living only for today, confronted with the reality that death is the end. It is messed up! Nothing makes sense. Nothing seems worth it. We have no hope!"

DESIGNED FOR MORE

Earlier in Ecclesiastes, Solomon states that God has placed eternity in the human heart (3:11). Humans are hardwired for hope and the only hope strong enough is the hope of heaven. That's why the good news of the Gospel truly is good news. Thanks to the life, death, and resurrection of Christ, we no longer have to live hope-choked lives. What was an insurmountable problem for the wisest man who ever lived is a simple truth for followers of Jesus today. The eternity for which our hearts were designed is promised and available to believers in Jesus.

Most people seem to believe in heaven. A 2007 Gallup poll confirmed that 81 percent of Americans believe in heaven (and as further proof of natural optimism, only 69 percent believe in hell).[38] The hope born in Bethlehem, secured on the cross, announced by the apostles, recorded in the Bible, and declared by the church is now known to billions across the globe. The missing hope that caused people in Solomon's day to "live their own mad course" and not be more "careful to be good" has arrived and is available to all who seek it.

It would only seem logical, then, that 81 percent of us would be living for the future, rather than for today. However, a quick look around reveals this isn't the case. There still seems to be plenty of people choosing their own mad course and not being particularly concerned about what they do, let alone trying to live for good. Which begs the question: Where's the gap? Why aren't more people living like they've won the ultimate eternal lottery?

We seem much more content to live for the moment.

Maybe you heard about Mirlanda Williams, a woman who claimed to have a winning lottery ticket for a Mega Millions jackpot worth over $100 million. She lived like a queen for ten days based on telling everyone around her she had won. The only problem was she didn't really have the winning ticket.

She got swept up in the excitement and possibilities. At the very least, she had bought a ticket. She had skin in the game. Most of the 81 percent of us who believe in heaven don't live like we have skin in the game. We don't live with the exuberance, hope, and a lightness of spirit expected in the lives of people who have been given such a jaw-dropping reward. A big reason for this is we have trouble imagining the prize, let alone that we've already secured it.

Ask a person what they would do with a million dollars and all kinds of images come to mind. We can picture ourselves tearing up bills, driving away in a new car, and visiting a place we've always wanted to go. Ask people to imagine heaven and things get a bit fuzzier. A video crew from our church once went out on the Las Vegas Strip to ask people what heaven looks like and the immediate answer was always "a white space." When pressed further, people described heaven as "big," "peaceful," or simply, "whatever you make it to be."

A Google image-search of the word "heaven" offers up pictures of clouds, robed figures, and majestic staircases ascending into sunbeams. Jokes offer up the image of Saint Peter standing in front of pearly gates checking a large book on a marble podium. Oprah Winfrey was even quoted as saying, "My idea of Heaven is a great big baked potato and someone to share it with." Even if her statement was made in jest, it demonstrates the utter fuzziness of our view of heaven.

ALMOST PARADISE

One of the things I love about vacations is the anticipation. The more clearly I can picture the destination, the more I look forward to it. That's why many people return to the same summer spot year after year; they literally have a perfect picture of it in their mind and it makes the anticipation all the sweeter. This is why the most expensive resorts and attractions spend so much money on brochures and websites. The more you can picture yourself at their spa, beach, or theme park, the more likely you are to visit.

The brochure most of us carry in our heads for heaven would never get a single visitor. If we were to combine the perceptions of the 81 percent who believe in heaven into an advertisement, it might be a little something like this:

> Heaven! Your eternity awaits...Ever wish you could escape into the sunny brilliance of a light beam? Ever wanted to float on a cloud? Well, now you can! God and His angels invite you to visit the ultimate-destination destination—Heaven!
>
> Peaceful bliss is just a cloud hop away. You'll enjoy activities such as singing, floating, and singing while floating. Every guest receives his or her very own harp and robe, which are yours to keep, well, forever. Be sure to enjoy the local sites of majestic white pillars and endless blue skies tinted slightly

purple...you might even run into some old
friends along the way. Just be back in time for the
main event, the Endless Church Service! The service begins at 8 sharp and never ends! With no
food, drink, sex, or sleep required, you are in for
one "righteously" good time! Don't delay!

This is the image I carried in my head a long time. The reality of heaven, our ultimate hope, never took root in my soul.
I was living the tragedy Solomon observed—a person living
without the true hope of heaven. This weak-kneed heaven
can't handle the weight of eternity. It's an anemic picture that
leads people to agree with Mark Twain when he said, "Go to
Heaven for the climate, Hell for the company."

When we live with a fuzzy image of heaven in our head,
our hearts begin to see more benefits in this life—maybe even
in hell, since that's where all the bad boys and party girls go.
This is why we need a clear reimagining of heaven. We need
to rewrite the brochure we carry around in our mind's eye
with full, glossy pictures of the place He has prepared. God
says Yes to life after this life, and the people who see this most
clearly often live with the most extraordinary hope.

DO YOU SEE WHAT I SEE?

The Apostle Paul wrote a letter to the church in Corinth
in which he mentions being "caught up" into heaven fifteen
years earlier. "Yes, only God knows whether I was in my body
or outside my body. But I do know that I was caught up to
paradise and heard things so astounding that they cannot be

expressed in words, things no human is allowed to tell" (2 Corinthians 12:3–4).

Paul doesn't offer much in the way of a physical description, but the experience left him with images more brilliant and beautiful than any Club Med brochure. Rather than make him want to sit around and wait for his ticket to be punched, this taste of heaven seemed to drive Paul forward in service to God. When things got difficult and his work didn't seem to be making a difference, I imagine Paul brought heaven to mind. It was also a source of great confidence. The whole reason Paul mentions his vision is to combat people who questioned his validity as an apostle. Having a clear view of heaven helped Paul forge the church ahead and live boldly for Christ.

The Bible offers a lot of symbolic imagery when discussing heaven. For instance, in the book of Revelation a heavenly city is described as being made of shining jewels, clear as crystal with streets paved with gold. There may very well be immaculate buildings all over heaven such as this, but the main thing being described is the glory and richness of God who lives in heaven. If you limit yourself to symbolic imagery, you miss out on the many other descriptions used throughout the Bible such as a house or mansion, a heavenly country, rest, a kingdom, a mountain, or a great feast.

All these analogies describe an aspect of heaven without giving a concrete photograph of what it is. Much of that is left to our imaginations. However, the imagery suggests that heaven will be a lot more similar to earth than most people imagine. We look forward to a new heaven and a new earth. And there is one word used by Paul in the passage above and by Jesus himself that's a bit easier to imagine than all the others...paradise.

Paul says he was, "caught up in Paradise." This is the same word used by Jesus as he turned to face the thief being crucified on the cross next to His. "I assure you, today you will be with me in paradise" (Luke 23:43). Ultimate hope in a short sentence.

What comes to mind when you consider the word "paradise"? When I hear the word, I immediately think of a beautiful, refreshing beach, lush with plants, cool breezes, and ocean air. And as it turns out, that's not too far off from the actual meaning. The Greek word *paradeisos*, which means "walled garden," was first used to describe elaborate gardens created for rich Middle Eastern rulers.

It was a place where the best that nature had to offer was cultivated to delight all the senses. Delectable fruits for eating, beautiful flowers of every color, birds chirping as the breeze wafts through the leaves of trees, carrying luscious aromas in the air. It was a place where you could simply rest, an oasis where you would walk and talk with friends; a protected, exclusive garden that refreshed your soul from the inside out. It was a place harkening back to the Garden of Eden. It was, well, paradise.

If this kind of place still seems a bit vague, let me help. To get your imagination flowing, look up the website for the Peter Island resort. Located in the British Virgin Islands, this destination offers crystal clear waters, swaying emerald palms, and unmatched luxury accommodations. If the cliff-top villas aren't exclusive enough for you, consider renting out the entire island—it's available by special request. I'm not saying heaven will look exactly like Peter Island, but I do know it's a much better picture of heaven than the one in most people's heads.

Another good way to capture the wonder of heaven is to think about what *won't* be there. Revelation 21 tells us heaven's a place with no sickness, pain, crying, or sorrow. Think about that for a moment. Can you imagine existing without those kinds of issues? We're assured that heaven is a place free of violence and injustice (Job 3:17, 2 Thessalonians 1:7). Heaven is a place where we no longer have to fear the tragedy of losing those we love (Luke 20:36).

Even on Peter Island you can fall and break your leg. There's a chance your bags could get lost or stolen on the way there. You could even get stung by a jellyfish, nibbled by a shark, or eat some bad shellfish and die. On earth, life is so uncertain—not so in heaven. It's like all the good things of earth with none of the bad.

The joy of holding a baby without the poopy diapers. The belonging of family without all the drama and past baggage. The majesty of a forest without all the mosquitoes. The glory of the ocean but no great white sharks. The promise of the Dallas Cowboys without all the losing. The pleasure of dessert without the bursting of buttons. The deep connection of a spouse without all the things that drive you crazy.

It may sound like a silly list, but it communicates a deep truth of heaven: it will be everything good in life, multiplied times God, minus all the pain, sorrow, fear, injustice, and loss. Every momentary delight you've felt in this life is just a fore-taste of what's in store. Every beautiful, lovable, wonderful thing you have experienced is just a hint of what Paul saw in his vision and what Jesus promised the thief. The joys we know today are shadows of the truer, deeper experiences that await us in paradise.

YOU 2.0

After life on earth, God says yes to our getting new bodies. Think of it as You version 2.0—the ultimate upgrade. The idea of getting a new body is not so exciting for young, physically fit people, but the older you get, the more you warm up to the idea. We collect aches, pains, and bodily malfunctions as we age. Knees start creaking, backs start hurting, and your brain gets fuzzy. You lose hair where you want it and grow hair where you don't need it (remember those gray nose hairs?).

Eventually you get to the point where the doctor stops trying to make you better and focuses on keeping you from getting worse. True, there is glory in aging. There's also quite a bit of humility. Once you've flipped the odometer on your body a few times, trading up to the new model doesn't sound so bad.

I bought my first new car when I was thirty-four. For many years I drove beaters. I was thankful for the cars at the time, glad they got me from point A to point B, but beyond that, I didn't enjoy driving. Finally the day came and I went all out. I drove into the dealership with a busted-down beater car and drove out in a bright red Mustang. For the first time in my life, I relished driving. I didn't care if I had to drive across town, because I got to drive across town in my Mustang!

That feeling of excitement, power, and newness of a brand-new car is just the smallest hint of how we're going to feel when we get our new bodies. And unlike my Mustang, we will never break down! The Bible says we'll be new, but still recognizable to each other. And we aren't just going to float around on clouds singing all day. I believe we'll have meaningful, productive work to do in our new bodies.

Furthermore, we'll live in new bodies, and this is what gets me really excited. The Bible says God created the current earth in seven days, but he's been planning the new earth since the beginning of time. Can you imagine how epic the new world is going to be? Picture your favorite vacation spot. Now imagine that God spent one thousand times longer working that up. Heaven is going to have Yosemite times one thousand; Hawaii times one thousand; Paris times one thousand; and Pebble Beach times one thousand. There are more beautiful places on this earth than any of us could ever visit, but on the new earth we'll have eternity to explore God's majesty and creativity. It's going to be awesome!

In the final book of *The Chronicles of Narnia: The Last Battle,* C. S. Lewis describes a scene at the end of time. The characters we have grown to love suddenly find themselves in a brand-new world that retains the best of the Old Narnia while being even better. They discover they can run without growing tired, and the farther they run, the more long-lost friends they meet. The emotion of the moment is captured in this short scene: "It was the Unicorn who summed up what everyone else was feeling. He stamped his right fore-hoof on the ground and neighed, and then cried: 'I have come home at last! This is my real country! I belong here. This is the land I have been looking for my whole life, though I never knew it till now. The reason we loved the old Narnia is that it looked a little like this.'"39

When we get to heaven and receive our new bodies, it will surely be the greatest moment of our existence, period. We will feel more at home and more alive than we ever dreamed possible. Everything good and lovely from this world will be present times one thousand in the next one. No matter how hard or difficult our time on this earth was, it will be swept up and forgotten in the beauty, wonder, and possibilities of the wonder laid before our brand-new eyes.

When I first read the scene from *The Last Battle,* it was the first time the promise of heaven went from a fuzzy image in my head to a solid picture in my heart. It was then I took my first toddling steps as a citizen of heaven, someone who carries a deep, hopeful picture of what Christ died to give us. And just like Paul, this clear picture of the future propels me into a life of faith and service where the message of God's grace is shared and the gift heaven is offered to as many people as possible. I remind myself daily to live with the hope of someone who has been promised the ultimate prize.

Do you know why the real winners of the Mega Millions lottery jackpot waited ten days to claim their prize, paving the way for Mirlanda William's week of fame? They were meeting with financial counselors and lawyers, trying to be as shrewd as possible with their winnings. They were well aware of the lottery curse, a phenomenon where people who win large sums of money wind up bankrupt in a few years. They wanted to get all their ducks in a row to protect their winnings from the hordes of scavengers that rise up to purloin lottery winnings. In the meantime, they hid in plain sight, telling no one of their windfall, living life as usual.

For ten days the three teachers went about their normal lives, going to work, fighting traffic, and doing laundry. Even though they tried to keep up appearances of a normal life, inside they had to be shouting with glee. I imagine the cost of a tank of gas didn't bum them out so much. The news of the day didn't seem so dire. The challenges faced at work didn't seem as soul-crushing as before. No matter what life brought their way, nothing could change the fact they were soon-to-be millionaires. All they were waiting for was the green light to claim the prize that was already theirs. They floated above the mire of everyday life, carried forward on the wings of imminent, definite reward.

What we hope for and look forward to shapes our lives. As followers of Christ, we have something far more valuable and permanent to look forward to than a lump of cash. A whole new body, a whole new world, and a glorious God in heaven awaits all who place their hope and trust in Christ. God says yes to life after our mortal bodies expire, and when you truly get a taste of the life to come, it makes this life all the more rich with purpose and enjoyment. We've received a gift that doesn't need to be hidden, a prize that multiplies rather than divides. A hope that will not fail.

As Solomon states, "Light is sweet; how pleasant to see a new day dawning" (Ecclesiastes 11:7). Because of Christ, a brand-new day has dawned when we have hope not only for this life, but also for the life we have in the paradise to come.

Chapter Ten

Yes to Life

There are only two ways to live your life. One is as
though nothing is a miracle. The other is as though
everything is a miracle.

—*Albert Einstein*

There are few moments of happiness more anticipated by
men than their honeymoon night. While their fiancées dream
up plans for the perfect dress, the perfect wedding, and the
most beautiful flowers, many guys can't help but focus on
what happens *after* the wedding. It's hard to blame them—it's
an epic moment.

My friend Chad was no different; in fact, he was slightly
worse. He and his wife, Sara, became Christians and met after
their first marriages had ended. They dated for two years and
finally tied the knot. Even though their past baggage made
it difficult, they remained celibate all through their dating to
honor their faith. Finally, the night arrived when they were
husband and wife, and the first thing they did was...*eat a
cheeseburger?*

It had been a long day, with a great reception that seemed to go on forever—with no time to eat as they greeted guests and mingled before changing and leaving. Then a limo ride where they realized they'd lost a bag while rushing to their flight with no meal service. When they finally reached their honeymoon suite, the couple was eat-your-arm starving. With their newfound freedom on the most anticipated night of their life, the thing the newlyweds craved most was a juicy, delicious cheeseburger. And to hear them describe it, they ended up ordering one epic cheeseburger!

SAVOR THE FLAVOR

There's a lot of joy to be found in the big moments of life. There's even more to be found in the small things. Ask people about the happiest times in their lives and they will most likely pause, search their minds a second or two, and mention a significant event in their lives. The day they were married. The day their child was born. The day they graduated from college. The day they surrendered to God. These are moments of happiness for sure, supercharged by their rarity and significance.

Then ask these same people what makes them the happiest and you're likely to get simple answers. They'll reply with things like good meals with family and friends, pursuing hobbies, catching a movie, watching a ball game, or listening to music. The list of simple pleasures is long and varied, but everyone seems to have their favorites.

We attach great significance to the big things in life, but often struggle to remember the last simple thing we did that made us happy. The big moments are planned for, cultivated, celebrated, and remembered. Like a wedding or a holiday, they carry the burden of large (and sometimes unattainable) expectations. But they're almost always memorable. The little moments, however, often drift away in a sea of commonness. As Solomon points out in Ecclesiastes, the little pleasures must be savored if we want to enjoy our lives to the fullest.

God doesn't just say yes to the big things in our lives, He also says yes to the small things. In the long run the amount of joy we get from the big moments is small compared to the combined joy we get from moments too small to remember. To maximize living in God's yes, we need to treat the small stuff with the same care as the epic moments of life. Enjoy the cheeseburgers in addition to the honeymoon. Those small details are often what made the large events of our lives memorable.

WEIGHT OF THE WORLD

Solomon challenges his listeners to soak up all the joy of the small stuff: "And this is not all that is meaningless in our world. In this life, good people are often treated as though they were wicked, and wicked people are often treated as though they were good. This is so meaningless! So I recommend having fun, because there is nothing better for people in this world than to eat, drink, and enjoy life. That way they will experience some happiness along with all the hard work God gives them under the sun" (Ecclesiastes 8:14–15).

In his first breath, Solomon mentions a horrible problem. He has seen that good people don't always get the credit and rewards they have earned. Sometimes they even get the punishment that wicked people deserve. In the meantime, the wicked not only go unpunished, but they're treated with the honor and accolades that the good people should have gotten.

It reminds me of the plot to *The Shawshank Redemption*, a film in which the hero, Andy Dufrain, is put in prison for a crime he didn't commit. Even when the true murderer is found, a crooked warden kills the only living witness, keeping poor Andy in prison to continue cooking the books of a scandalous side business the warden is running.

Something about this story makes our blood boil. We can't wait for Andy to escape and stick it to the warden. Our heart cries out for justice. Finally at the end of the movie, Andy escapes to a beautiful beach and the warden is revealed for the evil man he is. We revel in joy and relief because the good and the wicked are finally getting what they deserve. The truth triumphs and justice prevails.

The scene Solomon describes in Ecclesiastes 8 doesn't have a satisfying Hollywood ending. It ends in frustrating despair. Andy is still in prison. The warden is still receiving bribes and breaking the law. Evil goes on winning while good gets handed its lunch. It's deeply unfair and dissatisfying. It's exactly the kind of huge issue that can keep us up at night. What do we do in the face of such massive injustice? How do we cope with a world gone mad? Solomon recommends a two-word answer: "Have fun."

At first it sounds so trite, so absurd as to be laughable. *Have fun?* What good is that? According to Sonja Lyubomirsky in her book, *The How of Happiness*, having fun makes a bigger difference than you might think. In particular, the discipline of savoring moments has measurable positive effects. She writes, "Whether it involves a focus on the long ago, the present moment, or future times, the habit of savoring has been shown in empirical research to be related to intense and frequent happiness. Moreover, savoring is associated with many other positive characteristics. For example, in several studies people who are inclined to savor were found to be more self-confident, extraverted, and gratified and less hopeless and neurotic."[40]

Savoring is defined as the intentional prolonged enjoyment of everyday wonders. Rather than rushing through the day, you slow down and appreciate the gifts it offers. Rather than just hurriedly consuming, rushing from one demand to the next, you take time to savor. The sensation of cold water running down your throat on a hot, sweltering day. The sound of children's laughter from the playground. Discovering a new favorite song on the radio. Tasting the flavor of a sweet, ripe peach. Seeing the love in the translucent color of your spouse's eyes. Simply being alive to the present moment and all it offers.

STOLEN MOMENTS

Once again, the timeless wisdom of Solomon has scientific verification. People who consciously take time to savor the simple pleasures in life lead happier, more positive lives. It's not just wishful thinking; it's observable truth. When you take time to appreciate the small stuff, life gets better. After all, it is all a gift from God.

It means sitting down with that first cup of morning coffee, taking in the aroma and having a moment as you pray, reflect, and drink in the quiet of the morning. It means being refreshed, rather than rushed in the shower, enjoying the soothing flow of hot water. It means noticing the trees, clouds, and sky when you're out driving. You intentionally look for, and delight in, the hints of God you see in His creation—even when traffic is backed up.

It may sound like overly simplistic, pie-in-the-sky, warm, fuzzy nonsense, but the benefits of savoring have been continually demonstrated by empirical research. Lyubomirsky references two additional studies into the power of savoring. The first asked depressed participants to take a few moments each day to relish something they usually rushed through, such as a shower, a meal, or a walk, and then later write it down. In a second study, healthy students and community members were told to savor two pleasurable experiences per day by reflecting for two to three minutes, making the pleasure last as long as possible. According to Lyubomirsky: "In all these studies those participants prompted to practice savoring regularly showed significant increases in happiness and reductions in depression."[41]

This is why Solomon implores his listeners to cherish the small things. To eat, drink, and enjoy life, even in the face of such big things as social injustice, because the path to an unhappy life, and the paralyzing effect of depression, is greased with the thoughtless, thankless rushed consumption of everyday pleasures. We need to be intentional about savoring the small stuff because it easily gets lost in the busyness of life. When we remain trapped in our emotions or lost in doubt, worry, and frustration, we lose touch with what's right in front of us.

A neighborhood near where I live had a rash of robberies not long ago. In all, more than two-dozen homes were hit with tens of thousands of dollars' worth of items stolen; yet not a single police report was ever filed. The burglar was using an ingenious strategy, which allowed him to move from home to home over several weeks without being detected. What was his plan? He never stole anything big.

He slipped into houses and stole the small valuable items nobody would notice missing such as small amounts of cash, seldom worn jewelry, and the camcorder you only pull out at special events. He walked past thousand-dollar TVs, computers, and wedding rings because those items were noticeable and would prompt a call to alert the authorities. He also took unlikely items, such as an expensive vacuum cleaner. The people figured they'd loaned it to a friend or misplaced it, because who on earth would steal a vacuum?

Little did any of them know that the vacuum along with all the other items, including an heirloom necklace passed down for generations, sat in a pawn shop down the street waiting to be sold to whoever came by.

This small-time burglar was caught only because someone noticed a strange man lurking in a neighbor's empty house. When the police caught the man, he offered a full confession. As the slow process of notification began, people were shocked and shaken to learn that not only had someone been in their home, but also that something small had been stolen. Most of them had no idea items were missing.

Eventually all the stolen goods were returned, including

the vacuum, but something else returned to the neighborhood as well: a newfound appreciation for the small things. Take them for granted and one day they might come up missing.

HALF-FULL

Solomon mentions two roadblocks to appreciating the little things in life. The first is what I call the "Big Concerns" category. Notice how he starts his statement: "In this life, good people are often treated as though they were wicked, and wicked people are often treated as though they were good. This is so meaningless!" (Ecclesiastes 8:14).

He begins with a huge, complicated issue that governments, organizations, and individuals have struggled with for centuries: social justice. It's not simply a problem that can be solved with power and influence—if so, Solomon had both of those qualities in spades and could have brought about justice by kingly decree. The problem goes deeper than that. Life was horribly unjust but also beyond his influence. He wrestled with it. He couldn't understand. It kept him up nights.

Having passion for a cause is a good thing. We all need to wrestle with the deeper issues of life and how we can make a difference. We all have to consider the big concerns we face in the world, but we can't take so much weight and worry on ourselves that it crushes out the little joys in our lives.

Have you ever noticed that sometimes the people most committed to changing the world are the least easy to be around? There's a weight on their backs that seems to snuff out all joy. Every concern weighs on them so heavily that their lives become all about bearing big things rather than appreciating little things.

The same is true of people who are stridently focused on changing their personal world. Through sheer effort they march toward some life goal, to hit a certain weight, have a certain job, or meet and marry a specific person. They become so consumed with achieving that one big thing, or making that one huge change, that nothing else seems to matter, especially the little things. As for enjoying life, they seem to think, "I'll do that once I meet my goal, change my life, or change the world."

These are noble, admirable traits. Setting and achieving goals is something everyone should do, but please don't think that lasting happiness is found at the end of a major life achievement or world advancement. Solomon and research both say otherwise.

In fact, researchers have found evidence that the human potential for happiness is broken into three simple categories: (1) a set point (your genetic baseline level of happiness), (2) your circumstances, and (3) intentional activity.[42]

Most people think the greatest advances for happiness lie in changing or affecting that second category. If we could just change our life circumstances—the big things like our family, our job, our home, our health, our finances—then we would be much, much happier.

A single person thinks marriage will complete their lives and bring total satisfaction. A middle-aged woman longs for plastic surgery to finally feel good about her body. A young couple yearns for the freedom and happiness of wealth. An aging man battling a chronic knee injury believes the right doctor with the perfect procedure could solve all his misery.

We tend to put a lot of hope in big changes. And we spend a great deal of time and energy trying to control and change our circumstances. Although marriage, plastic surgery, money, and healing can bring temporary change, their potential to increase lasting happiness is very small. Social researchers believe it's a mere 10 percent. They've found that our biological set point for happiness accounts for 50 percent of our contentment but circumstances only account for 10 percent.[43] This means you can invest all the resources you have in improving the world and your lot in it, but it will only bump your happiness level up one point. Furthermore, you have very little control over many of your circumstances so depending on the big things for happiness is a frustrating proposition all the way around.

The best place to invest your time and energy to maximize happiness is in what researchers call "intentional activity." These include behaviors such as savoring sensual moments, being thankful, spending time with friends, and exercising regularly—in other words, the little things.

In fact, 40 percent of the happiness we feel is determined by how much we invest in and cultivate the small things in our life.[44] Better yet, the small things are completely under our control. We can choose every day, even every moment, to value the small things that bring happiness, and that happiness provides the healing, energy, and attitude to take on the big things.

SAME OLE, SAME OLE

The second thief that robs us of the small things is routine. Solomon describes this reality: "In my search for wisdom and in my observation of people's burdens here on earth, I discovered that there is ceaseless activity, day and night. I realized that no one can discover everything God is doing under the sun. Not even the wisest people discover everything, no matter what they claim" (Ecclesiastes 8:16–17).

These days it seems activity is more ceaseless than ever. I saw an infographic created by Domo, a business intelligence company, in which they pulled together research to capture all the data generated every minute on the Internet. Here are a few of the statistics that have only grown since my writing this:

Every Minute on the Internet
48 hours of new video uploaded to YouTube
571 new websites created
3,125 new photos added to Flickr
100,000 Tweets sent
684,478 pieces of content shared on Facebook
2,000,000 search queries typed into Google
204,166,667 e-mails sent

Each minute. Every minute. All day. All year.[45]
I get exhausted just thinking about it. It's truly ceaseless activity, just like Solomon described (and I'm pretty sure most of those e-mails land in my in-box during vacation). The endless activity has a way of washing away the wonder

of small things that can have such a lasting positive effect on our life.

How did we become so overwhelmed? And consumed by so many demands that leave us precious little time to enjoy what we have?

Think about the first time you drove by yourself. The freedom was intoxicating—just you, the car, and the open road. The possibilities were endless! Now think about the last time you drove a car (something inconceivable to people just a century ago): How was it? Were you thrilled with wonder? Were you thankful for the conveyance and delighted by the convenience? Or was it the same ole, same ole? Was it just a part of your ceaseless activity?

Psychologists have a name for the diminishing pleasure we receive from the small things of life. It's called "hedonistic adaptation," and it's a powerful force in both individuals and society. Whenever something good and wonderful happens, hedonistic adaptation comes along to steamroll the goodness into the fabric of our lives. What once was an amazing advancement becomes an expectation.

Comedian Lewis C. K. has gotten a lot of laughs off the concept of hedonistic adaptation in a routine called, "Everything's Amazing and Nobody's Happy." On the *Late Show,* he said, "I was on an airplane and there was high speed internet on the airplane...it's fast, I'm watching YouTube clips, I'm on an airplane. It breaks down, they apologize, and the guy next to me is like 'This is bull!' Like how quickly the world owes him something he knew existed only ten seconds ago?"[46]

He goes on to describe the whining and complaining on board another airplane after forty minutes of ground delays:

"Oh really, what happened next, did you fly through the air incredibly, like a bird? Did you partake in the miracle of human flight, you non-contributing zero? You're flying! It's amazing! Everybody on every plane should be constantly going ... 'wow!' You're sitting in a chair in the sky."[47]

How many little things do we do each day, how many "chairs in the sky" have we overlooked and reduced to the status quo? That text from a friend, the hand of our spouse, the love of our family, the comfort of air-conditioning, or the taste of a turkey sandwich. Not to mention the limitless grace and unconditional love of God!

The curse of the common plagues us every morning when we open our eyes and renders us immune to the simple pleasures that await. Even though there is ceaseless activity under the sun, we can make a conscious choice to step out of the flow and enjoy the good things God has given. When we do, we not only experience more lasting happiness, but reflect more of God's heart.

God is in the small stuff, and you should be, too. Don't let the ceaseless activity or the big worrisome issues of life rob you of joy found all around. With enough prayer and intentionality, you can literally increase your happiness by 40 percent by taking Solomon's advice and simply choosing to savor the moments and enjoy life.

EVERYDAY WONDERS

This past year we lost Lori's wedding ring. It is the ring that I bought her over fifteen years ago, and while it wasn't that expensive, it means a lot to us. The diamond had been cracked down through the center, but I kept putting off fixing it. I just took it for granted.

We searched for hours and hours. We emptied trash bags. We looked in every crack and crevice of the house. My son, Ethan, remembered seeing the ring and said, "I might have put it somewhere," but he couldn't remember where.

Finally, we were all exhausted. Lori was crying. My daughter, Emma, was crying. Ethan was hiding, and I was totally frustrated. Then for no particular reason, I grabbed a little pen holder, took the pens out, looked inside, and there it was.

I immediately called Ethan into the room, and he said, "That's where I put it! I remember now!" I was just so glad we found it that I forgot to be upset with him. Nothing else really mattered because we had found the ring! After we found it, I took it to a jeweler and got a new, unbroken diamond for it. No more taking it for granted.

The same can be true of your faith. It is easy to take it for granted. But what if it was gone? What if Christ had never come into our world? What if He had never lived, died, and risen again from the dead? What if there wasn't the church? What if I had never experienced the gift of forgiveness and grace? What if I didn't have these kids around the house to hide things and forget?

I don't want to take it for granted. When I remember God's incredible mercy, nothing else matters nearly as much. All my little problems get placed back into perspective. Jesus is so much more valuable and important than a ring, or anything else that has been lost. And He is available today—for free, though it cost God a precious price in His son Jesus.

NO REGRETS

Inspiration and Chai is the blog of Bronnie Ware. For many years Bronnie worked with people in palliative care, comforting dying patients in the last three to twelve weeks of life. During her time with people in the final weeks and hours of life, the topic of regret often came up. Bronnie compiled all these regrets into five general responses.

1. I wish I'd had the courage to live a life true to myself, not the life others expected of me.
2. I wish I didn't work so hard.
3. I wish I had expressed more feelings.
4. I wish I stayed in touch with friends.
5. I wish I'd let myself be happier.[48]

Aside from the first category, which has to do more with courageous life direction, all these regrets are won or lost in the small stuff. It may seem flippant and simple to try and find happiness by smiling more often, laughing often, holding hands, and enjoying the simple pleasures, but the small stuff escaped many people who came under Bronnie Ware's care and that represented their deepest regrets.

God says yes to happiness and enjoyment, and wants us to savor every moment, even in hard circumstances and big events beyond our control. Our world is filled with ceaseless activity, and we can easily drown in a flood of responsibilities, burdens, disappointments, and doubts. Or we can eat and drink and enjoy our work and cherish our loved ones and take control of our time each day to savor the special moments.

This is hard-won wisdom that we are foolish to take lightly, wisdom that is reflected in the words of writer Robert Brault: "Enjoy the little things, for one day you may look back and realize they were the big things."[49]

Making the yellow light. Holding hands with the person you love most. A warm towel straight from the dryer. An ice-cold drink on a scorching day. Juicy, ripe, fresh fruit. Two empty parking spots so you can pull through and face out. Noise-canceling headphones. Unexpected laughter. There's so much more small stuff I could mention. My list might be helpful, but what will be most helpful is the list *you* make. Do a good enough job writing down all the untapped moments of happiness and exercising the discipline of savoring, and pretty soon that list will be making you appreciate the many riches you experience each day.

Your Next Yes

Here now is my final conclusion: Fear God and
obey his commands, for this is everyone's duty.
—*Ecclesiastes 12:13*

A few years ago my best friend sent me a text message announcing that he and his wife were expecting a third child. I was excited for him and surprised as we had recently talked about how they weren't planning to have any more children.

I immediately called my wife and told her the news. We were thrilled and tried all day to catch him on the phone to celebrate the announcement. Later in the afternoon, I suddenly recalled a little detail of his life that left me confused. I sent him this text message, "Uh, didn't you have THE surgery? How was this possible?"

His reply, "April Fool's!"

I felt so completely duped. One word formed in my mind...*jerk!* I totally forgot it was April 1. He's done this to me several years about different things, including one year he told me they were filing for bankruptcy, and again, I believed him! Having been burned, I now walk around skeptical about what anybody says on April 1. I'm unwilling to trust them again until April 2.

Have you ever secretly wondered if God is playing an April Fool's joke on you? With all my talk about how God says yes to you, about how He can bring new meaning and contentment into life, do you still struggle to trust Him? Does it ever just feel like he's waffling between yes and no toward you? Do you *want* to believe, but still struggle to *rest* in this belief?

We've seen how God's yes can reinvigorate the little things in our lives. We've looked at how He brings satisfaction through pleasure, work, seasons, impact, friendship, contentment, wisdom, and the hope of heaven. God's yes to us is all over the pages of the Bible. Ecclesiastes has challenged us to realize there is no meaningful life outside of these yeses. We can wander and drift, like Solomon, but we'll end up in a place of confusion, frustration, and heartache. The question is: Will we trust Him and live in His promises? Will we take God at His word even when we are hurt and disappointed? Will we say yes to God in each moment and live in the incredible yes God declares to us in Jesus?

Just after Paul writes of God's yes, he reminds us of God's faithfulness: "For Jesus Christ, the Son of God, does not waver between 'Yes' and 'No.' He is the one whom Silas, Timothy, and I preached to you, and as God's ultimate 'Yes,' he always does what he says" (2 Corinthians 1:19).

If God's promises don't seem to be fulfilled when and how we think they should, we might be inclined to think that God is unpredictable or selfish. Sometimes, it could actually be that God is sparing us pain or shaping us for things we could never comprehend anyway. God's timing is perfect, and over and over in Scripture we are reminded that He is faithful to fulfill all of His promises. He follows through and does what He says He will do. Always.

Solomon went off the path with God and learned these lessons the hard way. As we've explored this jarring and meandering account of life and faith in Ecclesiastes, we've seen how God can bring meaning into our monotony. We looked at so many things He says yes to in our lives, things we can fully embrace through the power of His love and grace. We've seen that God isn't that roadblock, but the pathway to pleasure. He created us to serve Him, work for Him, and live with Him at the center. We've considered the importance of seasons and seen how critical it is to trust that God will make each season beautiful in His time.

Solomon concludes his survey of life in Ecclesiastes by bringing everything back to God. After all his zigzagging through the tragedies and follies of life under the sun, he implores his listeners to remember God each day. He writes, "Don't let the excitement of youth cause you to forget your Creator. Honor him in your youth before you grow old and say, 'Life is not pleasant anymore'" (12:1).

We've all heard the phrase "time flies." Older people are always telling younger people to slow down and appreciate what they have, because life "passes by in the blink of an eye." I can see for myself they were right. I've watched my kids grow from babies to preteens in what seems like a lot less time than twelve years. Someday I'll pick up this book, read my own words, and start bawling because my preteens are adults and have kids of their own. Time flies. And the older you get, the faster it goes. This is why Solomon urges us to be mindful of time and careful with youth. As we walk with God, He redeems not only our life, but our minutes, hours, and days. He gives us the perspective we need to make the most of our limited time.

THE AGE MAN SUIT

It's so easy to think we're going to be strong and healthy forever. It's hard to imagine not being full of mental and physical energy, especially in the prime of your life. That's why physicians at Berlin's Evangelical Geriatrics Centre have developed the Age Man Suit. Weighing in at twenty-one pounds, the Age Man Suit consists of a yellow face shield to blur your vision, ear protectors that stifle hearing, and knee and elbow pads that stiffen your joints. Medical students are required to wear the suit and perform simple tasks, such as walking up stairs and picking up coins in the hopes it teaches them empathy for their older patients.

Rahel Eckardt, a senior physician at the Centre, states, "My aim is to turn young energetic people into slow, creaking beings, temporarily at least. That way they will, I hope, develop a feeling for what it's like to be old."[50]

Solomon's words about aging are his attempt to put listeners in his own version of the Age Man Suit. He wants us to feel what it's like to not be as sharp, energetic, and strong as we are right now. And just like the students who gain a whole new appreciation for what it's like to be old, Solomon wants us to gain a whole new appreciation for what it's like to be young. Solomon wants us to say yes to life. He implores us to love God with all our heart, mind, soul, and strength before those resources are diminished.

Solomon continues: "Remember him before the light of the sun, moon, and stars is dim to your old eyes, and rain clouds continually darken your sky. Remember him before your legs—the guards of your house—start to tremble; and before your shoulders—the strong men—stoop. Remember him before your teeth—your few remaining servants—stop grinding; and before your eyes—the women looking through the windows—see dimly" (Ecclesiastes 12:2–3).

He so creatively describes the downsides of growing older that it sounds more like a reason to dread old age than to cherish youth. But the point isn't to fear what we will lose, but to cherish what we have. Rather than thinking of this as a picture of what we lose at the end of life, we need to think of it as the gifts we receive during this life. Gifts that are meant to be used as we remember our Creator.

Put on the Age Man Suit, read Solomon's warning, and then take it off. Feel the strength and vitality you have left, and invest in all of the opportunities God brings your way, because according to Solomon, our work and our passions are gifts as well.

YOUR NEXT YES

Solomon reminds us there will come a day when you can't say yes to new things. There will come a day when you have no more passion or desire. There will be a time when you are too old, weak, and out of it to live for God, but today is not that day! If you're reading this book, there is life left in you and God isn't done with you yet. You still have things to give and work to do. There are still purposes waiting to quicken your heart with fearless passion and fill your day with meaningful work. There are still people who need to hear from you, be helped by you, and be loved by God through you.

So what's it going to be? What's your next yes look like? Right now, today, what do you need to say yes to in your life? And think about it for a moment before you agree. Knowing what you need to say yes to and actually saying yes can sometimes be two different things. My kids will sometimes say to me, "Dad, I'm going to ask you something, but I want you to say yes first."

"Say yes to what?" I reply.

"To what I'm going to ask you," one of them will say, "just promise me you'll say yes." This is usually their way of getting me to agree to something they know I normally wouldn't approve, so I never answer them until I hear what they want!

But we can't fool God and fortunately we don't have to. He has already said yes to us in Jesus. He knows the big picture, watches our back, and protects our best interests. And each day He asks us to say yes to Him and to life.

It's a dangerous prayer to ask the question "God, what do you want me to say yes to today?" But it's even more dangerous not to. At the end of your life, as you reflect on all your experiences, relationships, and indelible moments, what do you hope to see? Will it be a celebration of a life well lived, or will it be poisoned by regret at all the things you wished you'd done? All the things you should have trusted God for? Will there be blank pages and desperate scribbles in the book of your life, or will each page be filled with God's design? Will each chapter look the same, over and over and over, or will it be bursting with risks and failures and God-sized dreams? Will it have been a life you never could have predicted?

Out of his wrestling match in Ecclesiastes, Solomon recognizes that all we have in this life is what God provides. Good food, productive work, loving relationships. Solomon wrestles with the glass being half-empty or half-full in this heartfelt monologue, and in the end, he concludes that despite how low our glass may seem in the moment, gratitude for what we have and an awareness of God's goodness will fill it up again. He writes:

> *Now all has been heard;*
> *here is the conclusion of the matter:*
> *Fear God and keep his commandments,*
> *for this is the duty of all mankind.*
> *For God will bring every deed into judgment,*
> *including every hidden thing,*
> *whether it is good or evil.*
>
> (Ecclesiastes 12:13–14)

This conclusion reminds us of our humanity—and of God's sovereignty, power, and holiness. It reminds us that there's always more in our glass than we're able to see.

Acknowledgments

The God of Yes represents the fulfillment of a long-term dream. Ever since God rocked my world with what it meant to live in His yes, I've wanted to write this book. The project idea lived in a growing number of computer files for so long that I had to convert them to current software or lose them! Thankfully, God makes everything beautiful in His time, and I was thrilled at the opportunity to bring this together. The process has been grueling at times, as all books are, and it was particularly challenging to work in a biblical book as layered as Ecclesiastes. I want to thank Shawn Wood, Jon Kohler, and Justin Jackson for insights that helped me keep one eye on the text and the other on the lives of readers.

Huge thanks go to the Hachette/FaithWords team for empowering me to see this dream come to fulfillment. For years I've known there were some books in me that I *had* to write. The Hachette/FaithWords team has not only believed in these books, but helped me bring two of them to life with *Pursued* and now *The God of Yes*. I feel so blessed to have the opportunity to work together and share such a personal and important message with a larger audience. Special thanks to Rolf Zettersten, Jana Burson, Shanon Stowe, and Harry Helm.

I appreciate the many people who helped behind the scenes, including Eugena Kelting, Drew Bodine, Kayla Gilmore, and Paul Mudd. Thanks to Esther Fedorkevich for being not only a great agent, but such an encourager through the writing and publishing process.

Of all the times I've hoped to hear "Yes," the one Lori shared with me on our engagement night will never be topped. Thank you for your faithfulness, love, and support through this process. You are such a gift from God. And thanks to Emma and Ethan for being such a joy to me. I can't imagine life without you, and I'm so grateful to be your dad!

Notes

1. Søren Kierkegaard, *Either/Or*, ed. and trans. by Howard V. Hong and Edna H. Hong (Princeton, NJ: Princeton University Press, 1987), 34.
2. Samuel Johnson, quoted in C. S. Lewis, *Mere Christianity* (New York: Macmillan Publishing Co., 1952), 78.
3. Stephen Hawking, quoted in Ravi Zacharias, *A Shattered Visage: The Real Face of Atheism* (Grand Rapids, MI: Baker Books, 1990), 13.
4. G. K. Chesterton, quoted in Dale Ahlquist, *G. K. Chesterton: The Apostle of Common Sense* (San Francisco: Ignatius Press, 2003), 16.
5. David J. Linden, *The Compass of Pleasure* (New York: Viking Penguin, 2011), Kindle edition, Chapter 1, paragraph 30.
6. Robert Galbraith Heath, as quoted in David J. Linden, *The Compass of Pleasure,* Kindle edition, Chapter 1, paragraph 11.
7. Linden, *The Compass of Pleasure,* Kindle edition, Prologue, paragraph 32.
8. "Survey: More Americans Unhappy at Work," CBSNews (January 5, 2010), http://www.cbsnews.com/2100-201_162-6056611.html.
9. Leland Ryken, James C. Wilhoit, and Tremper Longman III, eds., *Dictionary of Biblical Imagery* (Downers Grove, IL: InterVarsity Press, 1998), 965–66.
10. Andy Crouch, *Culture Making: Recovering Our Creative Calling* (Downers Grove, IL: InterVarsity Press, 2008), Kindle edition, Chapter 6, paragraph 5.
11. Ryken, Wilhoit, and Longman, *Dictionary of Biblical Imagery,* 965–66.
12. Tim Nelson, *Work Matters: Connecting Sunday Worship to Monday Work* (Wheaton, IL: Crossway, 2011), 26.

13. Seth Godin, "Slowly I Turned . . . Step by Step . . . Inch by Inch," *Fast Company* (May 2003), 72.

14. Iain Provan, *The NIV Application Commentary: Ecclesiastes/Song of Songs* (Grand Rapids, MI: Zondervan, 2001), 87.

15. Mark Buchanan, *Spiritual Rhythm: Being with Jesus Every Season of Your Soul* (Grand Rapids, MI: Zondervan, 2010), 18.

16. Max Lucado, *Fearless: Imagine Your Life Without Fear* (Nashville, TN: Thomas Nelson, 2009), 160.

17. Iain Provan, *The NIV Application Commentary: Ecclesiastes/Song of Songs* (Grand Rapids, MI: Zondervan, 2001), 103.

18. Dacher Kelter, "The Compassionate Instinct," *Greater Good: The Science of a Meaningful Life* (Spring 2004).

19. Scott Todd, *The Poor Will Not Always Be with Us* (Colorado Springs, CO: Compassion International, 2010), 30.

20. Joe Carter, "Texas Atheist 'Flabbergasted' by Outpouring of Christian Charity," The Gospel Coalition (March 22, 2010), http://thegospelcoalition.org/blogs/tgc/2012/03/22/texas-atheist-flabbergasted-by-outpouring-of-christian-charity.

21. Kerry Patterson, Joseph Grenny, David Maxfield, Rom McMillan, and Al Switzler, *Change Anything: The New Science of Personal Success* (New York: Business Plus, 2011), 86.

22. Ibid., 88.

23. Ibid., 43.

24. Carol Graham, "Happy Peasants and Miserable Millionaires: Happiness Research, Economics, and Public Policy," *VOX* (January 30, 2012), http://voxeu.org/index.php?q=node/4539.

25. C. S. Lewis, *Mere Christianity* (New York: Macmillan Publishing Co., 1952), 120.

26. Jeremiah Burroughs, *The Rare Jewel of Christian Contentment*, 42.

27. Ibid., 45.

28. Ibid., 47.

29. Ibid., 51.

30. Ibid., 65.

31. Paul Johnson, *Intellectuals* (New York: Harper Collins, 1988), Kindle edition, Chapter 1, paragraph 43.

32. Ibid., locations 609–11.

33. Ibid., locations 4785–86.

34. Ibid., locations 7103–10.

35. Gerald Clarke, "Harrison Ford: Stardom Time for a Bag of Bones," TIME magazine, February 25, 1985.

36. Raymond Novaco, "Anger as a Clinical and Social Problem," *Advances in the Study of Aggression* (New York: Academic Press, 1986), 2.

37. Joseph P. Simmons and Cade Massey, "Is Optimism Real?" *Journal of Experimental Psychology* (February 13, 2012), https://opimweb.wharton.upenn.edu/files/?whdmsaction=public:main.file&fileID=4107.

38. Frank Newport, "Americans More Likely to Believe in God Than the Devil, Heaven More Than Hell," Gallop News Service (June 13, 2007), http://www.gallup.com/poll/27877/americans-more-likely-believe-god-than-devil-heaven-more-than-hell.aspx.

39. C. S. Lewis, *The Chronicles of Narnia: The Last Battle* (New York: HarperTrophy, 1984), 213.

40. Sonja Lyubomirsky, *The How of Happiness: A New Approach to Getting the Life You Want* (New York: Penguin Group, 2007), 192.

41. Ibid., 194.

42. Ibid., 21.

43. Ibid.

44. Ibid.

45. "How Much Data Is Created Every Minute?" Domo Blog (June 8, 2012), http://www.domo.com/blog/2012/06/how-much-data-is-created-every-minute/.

46. Louis C. K., "Everything's Amazing and Nobody's Happy," YouTube, http://www.youtube.com/watch?v=8r1CZTLk-Gk.

47. Ibid.

48. Bronnie Ware, "Regrets of the Dying," *Inspiration and Chai* Blog, http://www.inspirationandchai.com/Regrets-of-the-Dying.html.

49. Robert Brault, "Who Wrote 'Enjoy the Little Things'?" *A Robert Brault Reader* (June 9, 2012), http://www.robertbrault.com/2011/04/who-wrote-enjoy-little-things.html.

50. Kate Connolly, "Suit Lets Medical Students Experience Symptoms of Old Age," *The Guardian* (July 9, 2012), http://www.guardian.co.uk/society/2012/jul/09/suit-students-experience-old-age.

About the Author

Jud Wilhite is a *New York Times* bestselling author, a speaker, and the senior pastor of Central Christian Church, a church founded in Las Vegas with multiple campuses, both national and international. Central is recognized as one of the largest and fastest-growing congregations in America. Jud is the author of several books, including *Pursued* and *Torn*. He and his wife, Lori, have two kids and live in the Las Vegas area.

For online service times, campus locations, or additional resources and media, visit centralonline.tv.